Two-Hour Dolls' Clothes

Two-Hour Dolls' Clothes

Anita Louise Crane

Sterling Publishing Co, Inc., New York
A Sterling/Chapelle Book

Chapelle Ltd.

Owner: Jo Packham

Editor: Linda Orton

Staff: Marie Barber, Ann Bear, Areta Bingham, Kass Burchett, Rebecca Christensen, Dana Durney, Holly Fuller, Marilyn Goff, Holly Hollingsworth, Shawn Hsu, Susan Jorgensen, Pauline Locke, Barbara Milburn, Karmen Quinney, Leslie Ridenour, Cindy Stoeckl

Photography: Kevin Dilley, photographer for Hazen Photography

Photo Stylist: Anita Louise Crane

Illustrations: Anita Louise Crane

THANK YOU TO PFAFF AMERICAN SALES CORPORATION for the wonderful sewing machine used to sew the designs in this book.

Pfaff American Sales Corporation
610 Winters Ave., P.O. Box 566
Paramus, New Jersey 07653-0566
(201) 262-7211

Gooseberry Hill Notions
1881 Old Lincoln Hwy.
Coalville, UT 84017
1-800-698-6576
*Antique and imported
lace and silk ribbons*

Library of Congress Cataloging-in-Publication Data

Crane, Anita Louise.
   Two-hour dolls' clothes / Anita Louise Crane.
      p.   cm.
   Includes index.
   ISBN 0-8069-3889-7
   1. Doll clothes--Patterns.   I. Title.
TT175.7.C73 1999
745.592'21--dc21
                                                    99-14088
                                                    CIP

10 9 8 7 6 5 4 3 2 1

A Sterling/Chapelle Book

Published by Sterling Publishing Company, Inc.
387 Park Avenue South, New York, NY 10016
© 1999 by Chapelle Ltd.
Distributed in Canada by Sterling Publishing
% Canadian Manda Group, One Atlantic Avenue, Suite 105
Toronto, Ontario, Canada M6K 3E7
Distributed in Great Britain and Europe by Cassell PLC
Wellington House, 125 Strand, London WC2R 0BB, England
Distributed in Australia by Capricorn Link (Australia) Pty Ltd.
P.O. Box 6651, Baulkham Hills, Business Centre, NSW 2153, Australia
Printed in the United States
All Rights Reserved

Sterling ISBN 0-8069-3889-7

If you have any questions or comments, please contact:

Chapelle Ltd., Inc.
P.O. Box 9252
Ogden, UT 84409

Phone: (801) 621-2777
FAX: (801) 621-2788
e-mail: Chapelle@aol.com

Anita Louise Crane has been designing, creating, photographing, painting, writing, and marketing since 1981.

Anita is best known for her original teddy bears. She has been a special-occasion and wedding dress designer and seamstress. In addtion, she has been an artist-in-residence and proprietor of The Bearlace Cottage in Colorado Springs, Colorado, and Park City, Utah, which featured her one-of-a-kind teddy bears as well as other collectibles, such as antique lace fashions, collectible antiques, laces, linens, and her paintings. She is an accomplished water-colorist.

She has written, photographed, and illustrated *Teddy Bear Magic, Making Adorable Teddy Bears,* and *Two-Hour Teddy Bears.* She has photographed a twelve-episode series called *The Life of Charlotte Bear* with her favorite creation "Daphney" playing the role of Charlotte, along with other teddy bear designs, for the Australian trade magazine *Dolls, Bears and Collectibles.* She has had featured articles in other trade magazines, which include *Romantic Homes, Teddy Bear and Friends, Huglets, Creative Needle,* and *Victoria.*

Anita lives in Park City, Utah, with her husband Bruce and kitty Raisen. Her other interests are designing and creating decorative items for her home, such as lamp shades, slip covers, window treatments, and decorative walls. Her home was featured in *Romantic Homes.* She likes to hike, ski, and snowshoe in the mountains.

I would like to dedicate this book to my brothers James and Butchie, and my sister Marie.

I would like to thank my editor, Linda Orton, for dedication and insight to each and every detail in this book. I could not have done it without her. I would also like to thank all the staff at Chapelle for making every book I do a fun project. Thank you, Jo Packham, for giving me the opportunity to express my artistic inspirations in each photograph, illustration, and pattern design. Thank you for using my cloth dolls and teddy bear characters to model the clothing in the photographs. A special thank-you to Kathy Pace of Coalville, Utah, for the loan of her lovely antique dolls to model my dress designs in the photographs, and for the lovely antiqued and imported laces and ribbons available from her catalogue.

Table of Contents

chapter 1

Essential Basics

Two-Hour Dolls' Clothes has been written so that any collector of dolls, from child to adult, and any level of seamstress, from beginner to advanced, can quickly sew beautiful clothing for their favorite dolls or stuffed animals.

Some of the garments pictured in the chapter openers are modifications of projects provided in the book. After you have completed a few of the projects, experiment by mixing different sleeve styles, skirt hems, flounces, and decorative trims such as buttons, ribbons, roses, ruffles, and pretty laces.

In the midst of today's hectic living styles, there still may be found a little time—even two hours—to sew up pretty doll clothes. Why not take the time to share and teach beginning sewing skills to your child or grandchild?

Basic sewing skills are all that are required. All garments have been designed so that even a novice can create beautiful heirloom doll clothes. Projects consist of patterns for play-clothes, suits, coveralls, and even dresses that are created from antique petticoats.

Before beginning, carefully review and follow the information contained in *Measuring Your Doll and Adjusting Patterns*. Take the time to review *Tracing and Transferring Patterns*, *Basic Sewing Instructions*, and *NoSew Instructions* in this section, and individual project instructions. Assemble all necessary fabric, notions, and tools before beginning.

Measuring Your Doll and Adjusting Patterns

Basic materials consist of:

Craft scissors
Pencil
Straight pins
Tape measure
Tracing paper
Transparent tape

The patterns in this book have been designed by doll height for 12", 14", 16", and 18" dolls. Body dimensions will vary from doll to doll. **It is imperative that you measure your doll's body proportions as well as height before starting.** A slim 18" doll may have the body proportions of the 14" pattern, while a soft full-bodied 14" doll could have the body proportions of an 18" doll.

Your doll's pattern size may be determined by measuring the following and comparing measurements to corresponding pattern pieces:

• Neck circumference plus seam allowance

• Chest circumference under armpit, plus seam allowance

• Arm length from shoulder to wrist, plus seam allowance and hem

• Waist circumference, plus 1"

• Length from waist to ankle, plus hem and waistband, or casing

• Length from neck to ankle, plus hem

Note: If your doll's measurements fall between two sizes, select the larger size. Do not mix pattern sizes.

Illustration #1a

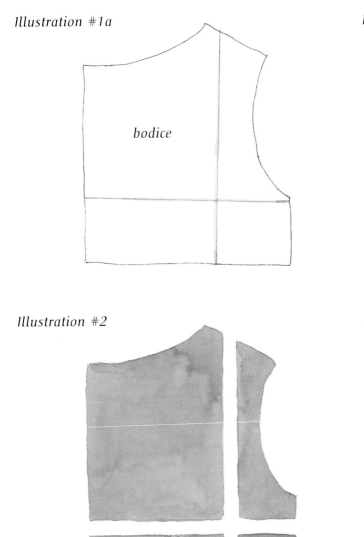

bodice

Illustration #1b

sleeve

Illustration #2

Illustration #3

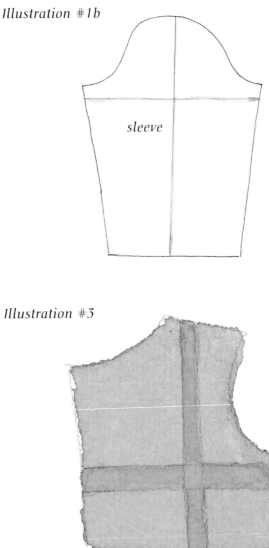

If the selected pattern size still requires modification, it is easily adjusted up or down in size if you use the following tips:

• Using a pencil and tracing paper, trace the selected size pattern. See Illustration #1a and Illustration #1b. Mark intersecting lines. Using craft scissors, cut the pattern along intersecting lines.

• See Illustration #2. Enlarge pattern by spreading pattern pieces apart on sheet

of tracing paper to doll's determined dimensions. Tape pieces in place, and trace.

• See Illustration #3. Decrease the pattern size by overlapping pattern pieces. Tape or trace resized patterns.

• Skirts and dresses may be lengthened or shortened by adding or decreasing length when cutting out or when hemming.

Tracing and Transferring Patterns

Basic materials consist of:

Pencil
Scissors: craft; fabric
Straight pins
Tape measure
Tracing paper

All patterns in this book are at 100% and represent the average size for a 12", 14", 16", and 18" doll. There are wide variations in doll body measurements, so you will need to keep your doll close by and measure before cutting out any patterns. Refer to *Measuring Your Doll and Adjusting Patterns* on page 9.

Using pencil, trace patterns onto tracing paper, tracing all marks and information.

Using craft scissors, cut patterns from paper and place on fabric, following instructions such as: place on fold, cut 2, and so on. Using straight pins, pin patterns to fabric. Using fabric scissors, cut out pattern pieces.

Patterns are not included for basic shapes, such as rectangles and strips. In these cases, the cutting dimensions are included. Using pencil and measuring tape, measure and mark necessary dimensions.

Cut or tear fabric, following the project instructions. *Note: Fabrics such as cottons and flannels will tear easily when a small cut is made. Fabrics such as wool, felt, polyester, and lace should be cut and not torn. Dimensions smaller than 2" should be cut and not torn.*

Basic Sewing Instructions

Basic materials consist of:

Fabric scissors
Iron and ironing board
Needle
Sewing machine
Straight pins
Tape measure
Thread
Velcro®

General Tips:

 All **seam allowances** and hems are ⅜" unless otherwise specified.

 When sewing doll clothes, **small stitches** provide the best results.

Sew **shoulder seams**, with right sides together. Using iron, press seams open.

See Illustration #1. **Cuffs** may be finished by hemming, adding lace, or adding a cuff.

Illustration #2

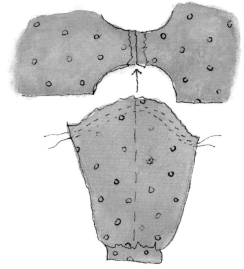

Illustration #1

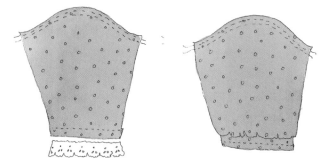

See Illustration #2. Sew **sleeves** to bodice by first finding top center of sleeve. Mark center by pressing a crease in the center of the sleeve or by marking with pencil or straight pin. *Note: Sleeve may be basted into place and then sewn.*

Neck edges may be finished in various ways:

Illustration #3a

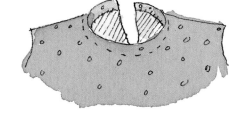

- See Illustration #3a. Fold neckline in and machine–stitch, hand–stitch, or fuse in place.

Illustration #3b

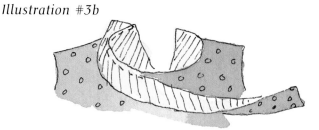

- See Illustration #3b. Cut a bias strip that is 1" wide x the length of pattern neckline. Sew bias strip to neck edge, with right sides together. Fold bias in half to inside neck edge, and sew in place.

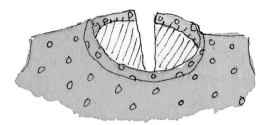

- See Illustration #3c. Sew or fuse lace to neck edge, with right sides together.

Illustration #3c

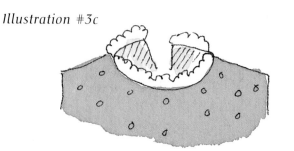

Illustration #4

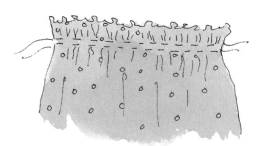

 See Illustration #4. **Gather** an area by sewing two rows of long stitches. Gently pull on bobbin (or bottom) threads, creating gathers. Using a needle and thread, gathering can also be done by hand. *Note: Use small machine-stitches if fine gathers are desired.*

 See Illustration #5. Sew **side seams** from outside edge of sleeve to bottom edge of bodice or shirt.

Illustration #5

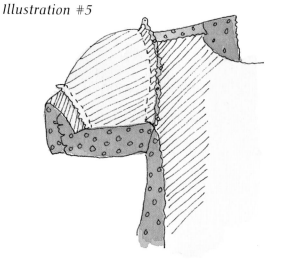

See Illustration #6a, and Illustration #6b. **Hem** skirt by folding edge under ⅜", unless otherwise specified, and machine-stitching, hand-stitching, or fusing in place. Hem can be finished by sewing or fusing lace to underside of skirt.

Illustration #6b

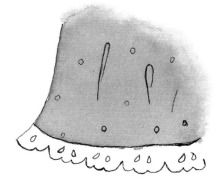

Illustration #6a

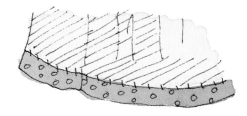

See Illustration #7a and Illustration #7b. Buttons and ribbons, Velcro tabs, hooks and eyes, and snaps are commonly used **closures** for doll clothes. *Note: Clothes may be permanently attached to a doll by sewing openings closed with tiny stitches after being placed on doll.*

Illustration #7b
Velcro® tabs

Illustration #7a
Buttons and ribbons

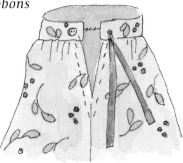

Note: Wrap ribbon around button and tie bow.

Stitch Guide

Overcast Stitch

Gathering Stitch

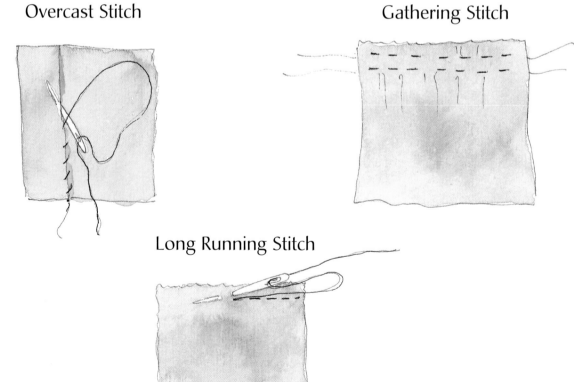

Long Running Stitch

NoSew Instructions

There are products available that can fuse and bond fabrics and eliminate sewing steps. It is within reason that an outfit can be finished with little or no sewing.

Basic materials consist of:

Damp cloth (for spills, sticky hands, and cleaning iron)
Fusible hem tape, fusible web, and/or fabric glue
Old iron
Paper towels
Press cloth or old cloth
Scissors: craft; fabric
Straight pins
Toothpicks

General Tips:

 Prewash fabrics to remove sizing so that fusible hem tape, fusible web, and fabric glues will fuse and bond.

Follow **manufacturer's instructions**. Instructions may vary from product to product. Use proper iron setting, following manufacturer's instructions. *Note: If iron is too hot, glue or fuse will melt and bonding will be unsuccessful.*

Test on scrap of fabric before using.

Gathering is best done by machine-stitching or hand-stitching.

Bonding consists of using fabric glues. Those glues that use heat to set seem to work best.

 **Fusing** consists of using fusible web or fusible hem tape that is set by heat.

When and how to use fusibles and fabric glues:

 Seams may be bonded or fused with fabric glue, fusible hem tape, or fusible web. Fusible hem tape is used most frequently. *Note: Iron smooth, flat side of fabric when fusing or bonding a gathered edge to a flat edge. Allow seam to cool, then test for proper bonding. Repeat if necessary.*

Trims and ribbons may be bonded or fused with fabric glue, fusible hem tape, or fusible web.

Appliqués may be bonded or fused with fabric glue or fusible web. Two-step fusible web works best because it is fused first to appliqué and then to desired placement.

 Hems and opening edges may be bonded or fused with fabric glue, fusible hem tape, or fusible web.

15

Designing New Fashions

The patterns in *Two-Hour Dolls' Clothes* have been designed in such a way that once you have mastered the art of assembly, you need only use your imagination to create new fashions.

The Alice pinafore can be sewn and worn over the Ellen dress. The sleeves from the Miss Dottie shirt may be just the look you desire for the Kim dress.

The combination of patterns and styles are limited only by your imagination. Not only can the patterns be combined, but the types of fab-

rics and decorative trims will make each design uniquely yours.

It is important that you measure your doll before selecting a pattern size. Avoid mixing pattern sizes as they will be incompatible.

Additionally, if you are designing and sewing clothes for a child's doll, you will need to take into consideration the age of the child and the safety factors when you select embell-ishments and closures.

Have fun, relax, and enjoy the art of making custom doll clothes.

Create a dress, using the Miss Rosie dress pattern, with a contrasting fabric for the ruffle, pockets, and neckline. Cut the sleeves shorter, then trim with the contrasting fabric.

Attach decorative buttons of varying size down the front length of the dress.

Sew this party dress, using the Kim bodice pattern and skirt dimensions with the "A" Beatrix collar. Use a navy blue fabric for the bodice, sleeves, and skirt. Make the collar from a white fabric.

Trim the dress with white grosgrain ribbon, six tiny pink buttons attached to the sleeves, and a pink bow tied at the neck.

Sew a lovely dress, using the Miss Dottie sleeve pattern and the Miss Rosie bodice pattern and skirt dimensions.

Add decorative accents by sewing rows of lace to hem and front bodice. Trim sleeve cuff and neckline with lace. Attach small ribbon bows and silk roses to neckline, cuffs, and hem.

Create an elegant dress, using the Jennifer bodice and skirt pattern. Shorten the Miss Dottie sleeve pattern and add long cuffs.

Embellish with a purchased lace collar and wide lace at hemline. Attach string pearls draped like a garland around the skirt and to the edge of the cuffs. Tie small bows from wire-edged ribbon and attach to sleeves and pearl garland.

Cut out soft wool fabric, using the "A" Beatrix sleeve and duster patterns. Trim with fur for collar, cuffs, and hem.

Attach six contrasting colored buttons down front for accent.

Illustration #1

Sew an heirloom dress, cut out from an antique dress, using the Hollyhock bodice pattern and the Kim sleeve pattern. Make the skirt from the bottom of an antique dress as shown in Illustration #1.

chapter 1

Spring and

Summer Wear

Rose

Rose

All you will need are some pretty lace eyelet and soft ribbons to make this adorable pinafore apron. If you have a piece of antique eyelet, you can make a beautiful keepsake heirloom.

Notions:

Fusible hem tape (optional)
Lace: 8"–10"-wide with scalloped
    edge (1 yd.)
Ribbon: ¼"-wide satin (2 yd.)
Thread

Tools:

Fabric scissors
Iron and ironing board
Measuring tape
Sewing machine
Straight pins
Tracing paper and pencil

Instructions for Pinafore

1 Refer to *Essential Basics* on pages 8–15. Using patterns on pages 24–25, trace patterns onto tracing paper. Place and pin skirt pattern so bottom is on scalloped edge of lace. Place and pin bodice pattern above scalloped edge. Using fabric scissors, cut out pattern pieces.

2 Using sewing machine, sew shoulder seams, with right sides together. Using iron, press seams open.

3 Fold neck edge in ⅛" and press. Sew or fuse (referring to *NoSew Instructions* on page 15) neck edge hem in place. *Optional: ½"-wide lace may be sewn or fused to neck if desired.*

4 Fold armholes and center back edges of bodice in ⅛" and press. Fold side edges of all skirt pieces in ⅛" and press. Sew or fuse edges in place.

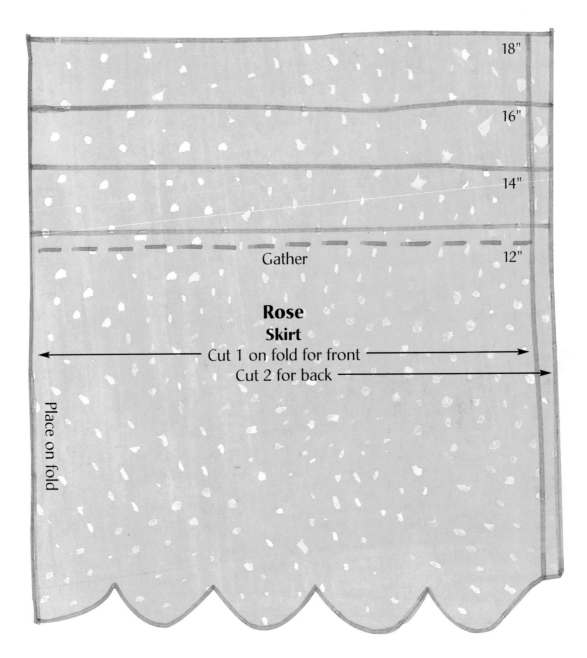

18"

16"

14"

Gather   12"

Rose
Skirt
← Cut 1 on fold for front →
Cut 2 for back →

Place on fold

Illustration #1

5 Sew top edge of all skirt pieces with gathering stitch. Pull bobbin thread to gather.

6 Sew skirt back pieces to back bodice. Sew skirt front piece to front bodice.

7 See Illustration #1. Cut eight 9" pieces of ribbon for ties. Sew ribbon to back, neck, and sides.

Alternative: Make a pinafore apron from a pretty printed fabric.

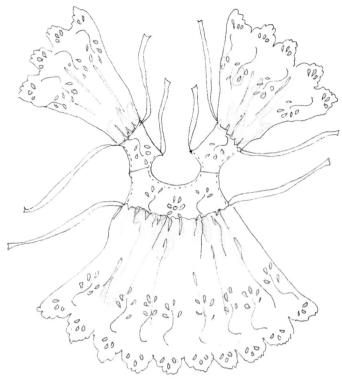

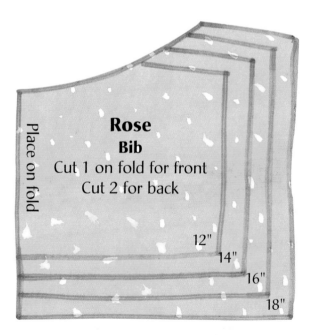

Place on fold

Rose
Bib
Cut 1 on fold for front
Cut 2 for back

12"
14"
16"
18"

Kim

Kim

The cute star-shaped buttons, available in rainbow colors, were the inspiration for this summer coat, which was stitched from a damask table napkin.

The dress is a simple design to complement the summer coat.

Fabric:

Fabric: cotton (½ yd.)
       cotton damask (½ yd.)

Notions:

Buttons: decorative (7)
        ½" (3)
Fusible hem tape (optional)
Thread
Velcro® tabs

Tools:

Fabric scissors
Iron and ironing board
Measuring tape
Sewing machine
Sewing needle
Straight pins
Tracing paper and pencil

Instructions for Dress and Coat

1 Refer to *Essential Basics* on pages 8–15. Using patterns on pages 29–32, trace patterns onto tracing paper. Place and pin dress pattern to cotton fabric. See Skirt Dimensions on page 29. Cut or tear rectangle for skirt. See Bias Dimensions on page 29. Using fabric scissors, cut bias strip for neckline. Place and pin coat pattern to cotton damask fabric. Cut two 2" x 3½" pieces for lapel lining. Cut out pattern pieces. See Cuff Dimensions on page 31. Cut out two rectangles for cuffs. See Pocket Dimensions on page 31. Cut out two rectangles for pockets.

Dress

1 Using sewing machine, sew shoulder seams, with right sides together. Using iron, press seams open.

2 Sew bias strip to neck edge, with right sides together. Fold bias strip in half to inside of neck edge and machine-stitch or hand-stitch in place.

3 Fold wrist end of sleeve in ½" and press. Machine-stitch, hand-stitch, or fuse (referring to *NoSew Instructions* on page 15) in place.

4 Sew running stitch across top of sleeve to help ease sleeve into armhole. Center and pin top of sleeve to shoulder seam, with right sides together. Sew from center out. Repeat for second sleeve.

5 Sew side seams of bodice and sleeves, with right sides together. Press seams open.

6 Sew top of skirt with two rows of gathering stitches. Pull bobbin threads to gather. Center and pin skirt to bodice, with right sides together. Sew in place.

7 Sew center back edges of skirt, with right sides together, stopping 2" below bodice.

8 Fold center back opening in ⅜" and press. Sew or fuse in place.

9 Using needle and thread, hand-stitch one ½" button at back neck edge, midway back bodice, and waist.

10 Cut six 6" ribbons. Machine-stitch or hand-stitch two ribbons opposite buttons on other side of bodice. Tie ribbons around buttons to secure dress.

11 Pin dress to desired length and press. Machine-stitch, hand-stitch, or fuse in place.

Bias Dimensions:

12"	5¼" x 1¼"
14"	6¼" x 1¼"
16"	8" x 1½"
18"	9½" x 1½"

Skirt Dimensions:

12"	24¼" x 6¾"
14"	28¼" x 7⅝"
16"	32⅛" x 8½"
18"	36" x 9½"

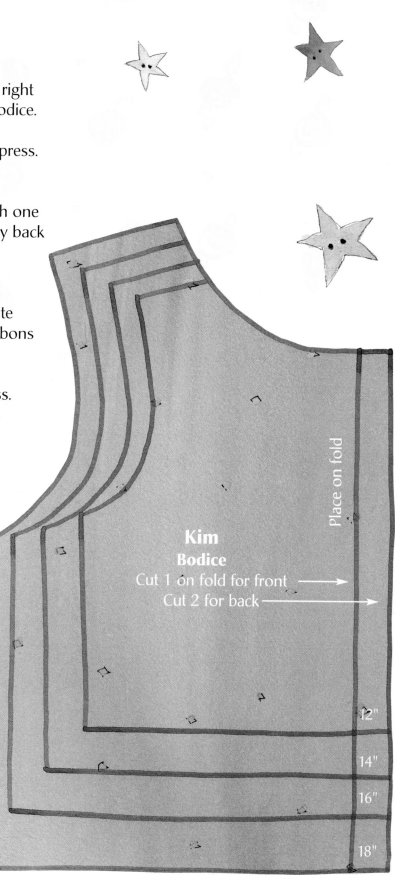

Place on fold

Kim
Bodice
Cut 1 on fold for front →
Cut 2 for back →

12"
14"
16"
18"

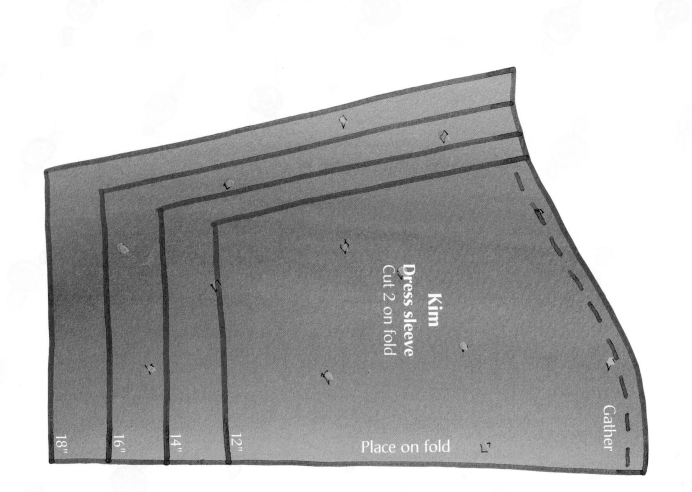

On the pattern piece (from largest to smallest): 18", 16", 14", 12"

Kim
Dress sleeve
Cut 2 on fold

Place on fold

Gather

Coat

1 Place and pin jacket lapel lining to jacket front, with right sides together, aligning with front edge. Using sewing machine, sew outside corner of lapel. Trim off excess fabric along neck edge. Turn right side out and press. Repeat for other side. Topstitch ¼" from edge around front opening and neck. Fold lapels back and press.

2 Fold all pocket edges in ⅛" and, using iron, press. Place and pin one pocket on each front section. Sew or fuse (referring to *NoSew Instructions* on page 15) in place.

3 Sew shoulder seams, with right sides together. Press shoulder seams flat.

4 Place and pin back dart. Sew in place. Fold back neck edge in ⅜". Machine-stitch or hand-stitch in place. *Optional: Sew lace hem tape to back neck edge and fold in. Machine-stitch or hand-stitch in place.*

5 Sew top and wrist end of sleeve with gathering stitch. Pull bobbin threads to gather.

6 Place and pin cuff to wrist end of sleeve. Sew in place. Fold cuff in half to inside of sleeve. Machine-stitch or hand-stitch in place.

7 Center and pin top of sleeve to shoulder seam, with right sides together. Sew from center out. Repeat for second sleeve.

8 Sew side seams and sleeves of jacket, with right sides together.

9 Sew lace hem tape to coat hem. Turn lace hem tape under and machine-stitch, hand-stitch, or fuse in place.

10 Using needle and thread, hand-stitch five decorative buttons to one side of coat. Hand-stitch decorative button to each pocket. Attach Velcro tabs to inside of coat for closure.

11 *Optional: Cut small square of cotton fabric. Fold and place in pocket. Sew in place.*

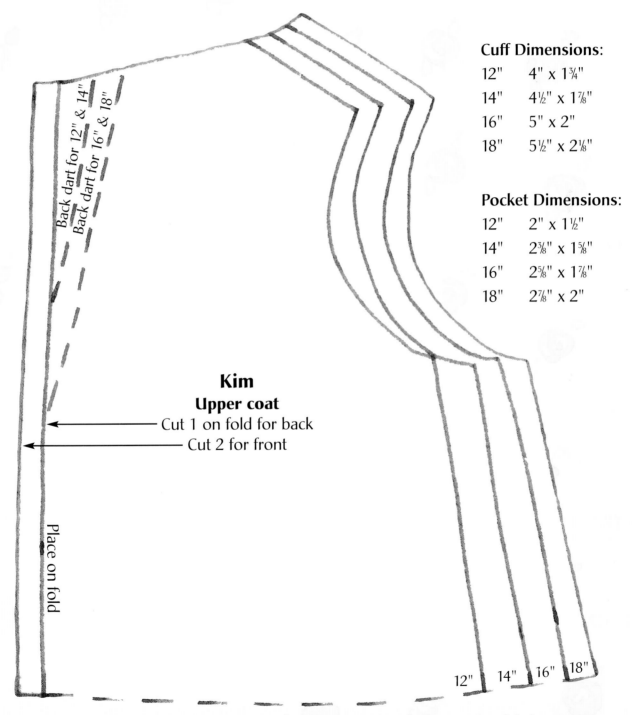

Cuff Dimensions:

12"	4" x 1¾"
14"	4½" x 1⅞"
16"	5" x 2"
18"	5½" x 2⅛"

Pocket Dimensions:

12"	2" x 1½"
14"	2⅜" x 1⅝"
16"	2⅝" x 1⅞"
18"	2⅞" x 2"

Back dart for 12" & 14"
Back dart for 16" & 18"

Kim
Upper coat
— Cut 1 on fold for back
— Cut 2 for front

Place on fold

12" 14" 16" 18"

Note: Tape upper coat pattern to lower coat pattern before cutting fabric.

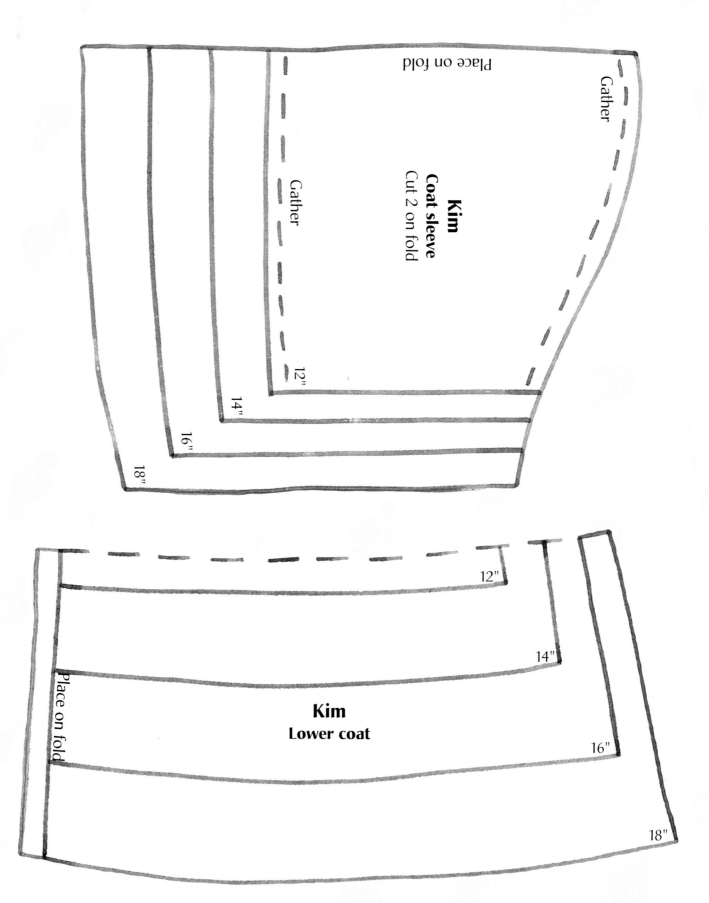

Place on fold

Gather

Kim
Coat sleeve
Cut 2 on fold

Gather

12"

14"

16"

18"

12"

14"

16"

18"

Place on fold

Kim
Lower coat

Note: Tape lower coat pattern to upper coat pattern before cutting fabric.

Hailey and Miss Hopper

Hailey

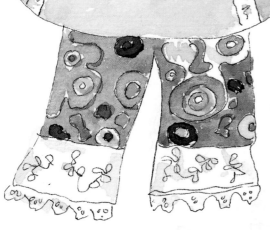

Every doll needs playclothes and they should be this fun. This cute top has an appliquéd turtle cut from the same fabric as the pants. You may choose to quilt around the turtle to accent the design. Look for fabrics with adorable prints that can be cut from the fabric and used as appliqués.

Fabric:

Fabric: cotton (¼ yd.)
cotton, pattern suitable for appliqué (¾ yd.)

Notions:

Buttons: ⅜" (5)
Drawstring (⅔ yd.)
Fusible bond paper
Fusible hem tape
Lace: ½"-wide (1¾ yds.)
3"-wide (½ yd.)
Low-loft quilt batting (scrap) (optional)
Thread
Velcro® tabs

Note: A smaller width lace than 3" may be desired for 12" and 14" dolls.

Tools:

Fabric scissors
Iron and ironing board
Measuring tape
Sewing machine
Sewing needle
Small safety pin
Straight pins
Tracing paper and pencil

Instructions for Shirt and Pants

1 Refer to *Essential Basics* on pages 8–15. Using patterns on pages 36–37, trace patterns onto tracing paper. Place and pin shirt pattern to ¼ yd. cotton fabric. Place and pin pants pattern to ¾ yd. patterned fabric. Using fabric scissors, cut out pattern pieces.

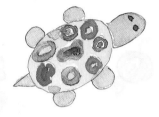

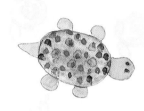

Shirt

1 Select appliqué motif from fabric. Cut square around selected motif that is ½" larger.

2 Refer to *NoSew Instructions* on page 15. Using iron, fuse appliqué to one side of fusible bond paper. Cut out appliqué motif. Remove paper backing from appliqué. Center appliqué on shirt front and fuse in place.

3 Place and pin ½" lace vertically 2" from center front on each side. Using sewing machine, sew in place. Place and pin lace horizontally 1¼" from bottom edge. Sew in place. Place and pin lace horizontally ¾" below neck edge, extending lace out to wrist edge. Sew in place.

4 *Optional: Using measuring tape, measure rectangle space inside lace. Cut quilt batting to measurements. Place or pin batting to inside of bodice behind appliqué. See Stitch Guide on page 14. Using needle and thread, hand-stitch a long running stitch around outside edge of batting. Quilt around outside of appliqué for added dimension and accent. Remove long running stitch.*

5 Sew shoulder and top sleeve seams, with right sides together. Using iron, press seams open.

6 Fold wrist end of sleeves in ⅜" and press. Sew or fuse, with fusible hem tape.

7 Fold neck edge in ⅛" and press. Sew in place. Sew ½"-wide lace to outside of neck edge, with right sides together.

8 Sew side and arm seams, with right sides together. Press seams open. Turn bottom edge of blouse under and press. Sew or fuse in place.

9 Fold center back opening in ½" and press. Sew or fuse in place.

10 Attach Velcro tabs to center back opening for closure. Using needle and thread, hand-stitch buttons to center back opening for accent.

✔ *Two-hour assembly is based on sewing time of finished shirt and not on quilting time. This shirt may require extra time for quilting.*

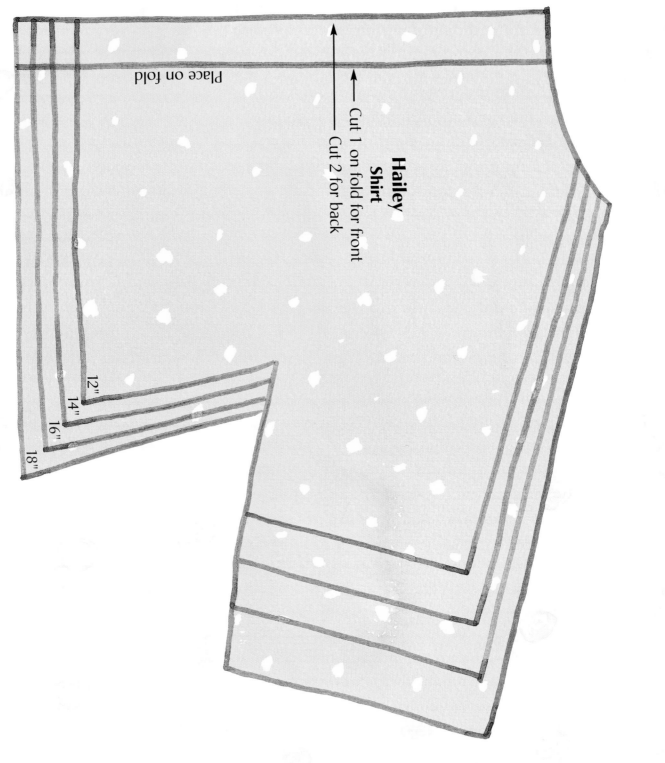

Place on fold

**Hailey
Shirt**

Cut 1 on fold for front
Cut 2 for back

12"
14"
16"
18"

Pants

1 Fold bottom leg edge in ½" and, using sewing machine, sew in place. Sew 3"-wide lace to outside of bottom leg edge, with right sides together.

2 Sew front seam from "A" to "B", with right sides together. Repeat with back seam. Sew inside leg seam, with right sides together.

3 Fold top of pants in 1" and press. Sew casing around top of pants ¼" from raw edge, leaving 1" opening at back seam for drawstring.

Attach safety pin to drawstring and push through casing. Place pants on doll and pull drawstring to fit waist. Tie in bow.

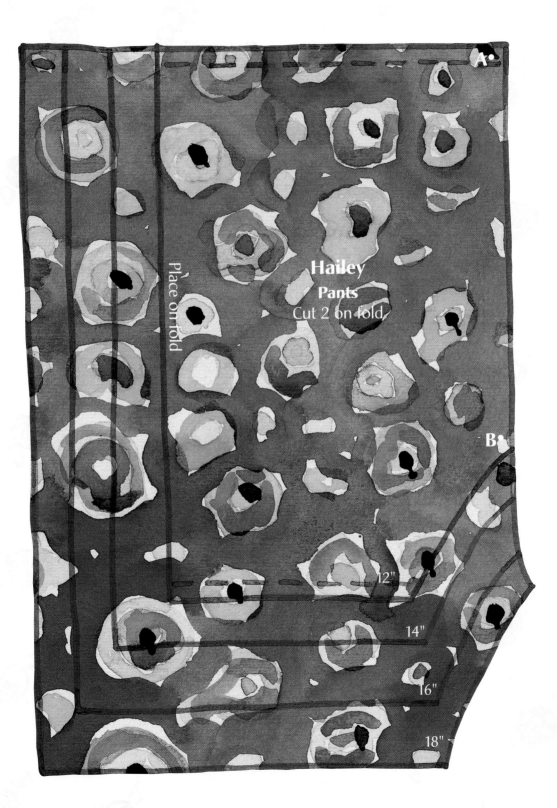

Miss Hopper

What could be more delightful than playclothes sewn from colorful fabrics with grasshoppers, ladybugs, and polka dots? You will not be able to resist purchasing quarter-yards of such wonderfully contrasting fabrics to sew playclothes.

Fabric:

Fabric: cotton, four contrasting patterns (¼ yd. each)
cotton (scrap)

Notions:

Buttons: ¾" novelty (3)
⅜" (1)
Drawstring (⅔ yd.)
Embroidery floss
Fusible hem tape (optional)
Ribbon: ⅛"-wide satin (⅓ yd.)
Snaps (3)
Thread
Yarn

Tools:

Fabric scissors
Iron and ironing board
Measuring tape
Sewing machine
Sewing needle
Straight pins
Tracing paper and pencil

Instructions for shirt, skirt, and pants

1 Refer to *Essential Basics* on pages 8–15. Using patterns on pages 39, 40, and 42, trace patterns onto tracing paper. Place and pin shirt bodice to ¼ yd. cotton fabric. See Sleeve Ruffle Dimensions on page 40. Cut or tear two strips for sleeve ruffles from ¼ yd. contrasting fabric. See Skirt Dimensions on page 41. Cut or tear rectangle for skirt from ¼ yd. contrasting fabric.

Using measuring tape, determine doll waist circumference, plus 1". Using fabric scissors, cut one 2"-wide strip to these dimensions for skirt waistband. Place and pin pants pattern to remaining ¼ yd. cotton fabric. See Pant Ruffle Dimensions on page 41. Cut or tear two rectangles for pant ruffles from scrap fabric. Cut out pattern pieces.

Shirt

1 See Illustration #1a on page 40. Using sewing machine, sew bodice fronts together by sewing from each shoulder along neck edge, down front, and along bottom edge of bodice to side, with right sides together. Turn right side out and, using iron, press flat.

2 See Illustration #1b on page 40. Sew bodice backs together by sewing around top of neck edge to shoulder seams, with right sides together. Sew bottom edges together. Turn right side out and press.

3 Sew front and back shoulder seams, with right sides together. Press seams open.

4 Fold one long edge of sleeve ruffle in ½" and press. Stitch or fuse (referring to *NoSew Instructions* on page 15) in place. Repeat with other ruffle. Sew raw edges with gathering stitch. Pull bobbin thread to gather.

Place on fold

Miss Hopper
Bodice back
Cut 2 on fold

12" 14" 16" 18"

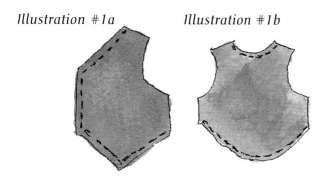

Illustration #1a　　　*Illustration #1b*

5 Place and pin ruffle to shoulder edge, with right sides together. Sew from center out. Repeat with other ruffle.

6 Sew side seams and sleeves, with right sides together. Press seams open.

7 Attach snaps down front edge for closures. Using needle and embroidery floss, hand-stitch on novelty buttons, tying knot in front. Trim floss ends ½" from knot.

Sleeve Ruffle Dimensions:

12"	8½" x 2⅜"
14"	9½" x 2⅝"
16"	10¾" x 2⅞"
18"	12" x 3"

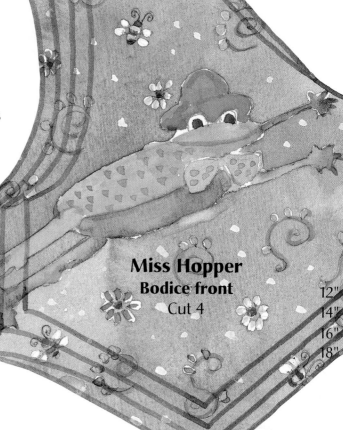

Miss Hopper
Bodice front
Cut 4

12"
14"
16"
18"

Skirt

1 Fold one long edge of skirt in ½" and using iron, press to hold. Using sewing machine, sew in place. *Optional: Refer to NoSew Instructions on page 15. Fuse with fusible hem tape.*

2 Sew raw edge with gathering stitch. Pull bobbin thread to gather.

3 Place and pin waistband to gathered waist. Sew in place. Fold waistband in half to inside of skirt, tucking the waistband ends inside, and press. Sew or fuse in place.

4 Sew back seam of skirt, with right sides together, stopping 2" below waist. Fold

opening of skirt and waistband in ⅜" and press. Machine-stitch, hand-stitch, or fuse in place.

5 Using needle and thread, sew ⅜" button to one end of waistband. Sew two 6" ribbons to opposite end of waistband. Tie ribbons around button to secure waist.

Skirt Dimensions:

12"	16¼" x 4⅝"
14"	18⅞" x 5⅜"
16"	21½" x 5⅞"
18"	24" x 6½"

Pants

1 Fold one long edge of each ruffle piece in ⅛" and, using iron, press. Using sewing machine, sew in place.

2 Sew raw edge of ruffles with gathering stitch. Pull bobbin thread to gather. Sew ruffle to leg bottom, with right sides together.

3 Sew front seam from "A" to "B" with right sides together. Repeat with back seam. Sew inside leg seam, with right sides together.

Pant Ruffle Dimensions:

12"	9" x 1½"
14"	10¼" x 1¾"
16"	11¾" x 2"
18"	13" x 2"

4 Fold top of pants in 1" and press. Sew casing around top of pants ¼" from raw edge, leaving 1" opening at back seam for drawstring.

Attach safety pin to drawstring and push through casing. Place pants on doll and pull drawstring to fit waist. Tie in bow.

A•

Miss Hopper
Pants
Cut 2 on fold

Place on fold

B•

12"

14"

16"

18"

Blossom

Blossom

A lovely piece of damask inspired this charming bed jacket. Pretty antique-style ribbons and lace add detail and romance. Explore your favorite fabric shop, and let beautiful ribbons and lace inspire your own version of this bed jacket.

Fabric:

Fabric: damask (¼ yd.)

Notions:

Braid: fine metallic (1 yd.)
Lace: ¾"-wide scalloped edge (½ yd.)
Ribbon: ½"-wide embroidered (½ yd.)
        ¾"-wide embroidered (1 yd.)
Thread

Tools:

Fabric glue
Fabric scissors
Iron and ironing board
Measuring tape
Sewing machine
Straight pins
Tracing paper and pencil

Instructions for Bed Jacket

1 Refer to *Essential Basics* on pages 8–15. Using pattern on page 45, trace pattern onto tracing paper. Place and pin jacket pattern to damask fabric. Using fabric scissors, cut out pattern pieces.

2 Using sewing machine, sew shoulder and upper sleeve seams, with right sides together. Using iron, press seams open.

3 Place and pin ½"-wide ribbon to wrist end of sleeves. Sew or fuse (referring to *NoSew Instructions* on page 15) in place.

4 Sew side of bodice and upper sleeve seams, with right sides together.

5 Place and pin ¾"-wide ribbon to neck, front, and bottom edge of jacket. Sew in place.

6 Using fabric glue, bond scalloped lace to underside of hem, allowing scalloped edge to show below hemline.

7 Cut two 18" pieces of metallic braids for ties. Fold metallic braid in half and sew to each side of neck for closure. *Optional: Ribbon may be used in place of braid.*

Blossom Bed jacket

Cut one on fold for back
Cut two for front

12"
14"
16"
18"

Place on fold

Liza

Liza

Bright colors and contrasting patterns create a timeless playsuit that looks as darling on your antique doll as it does on your child's favorite contemporary doll.

Fabric:

Fabric: cotton (¼ yd.)
       cotton (⅓ yd.)

Notions:

Buttons ⅜″ (2)
Fusible hem tape (optional)
Ribbon: ⅛″-wide satin (⅔ yd.)
Thread

Tools:

Fabric scissors
Iron and ironing board
Measuring tape
Sewing machine
Sewing needle
Straight pins
Tracing paper and pencil

Instructions for Playsuit

1 Refer to *Essential Basics* on pages 8–15. Using pattern on page 50, trace pattern onto tracing paper. Place and pin pants bottom pattern to ⅓ yd. cotton fabric. Using fabric scissors, cut out pattern pieces. See Strap Dimensions on page 49. Cut or tear two strips for straps. See Bib Dimensions on page 49. Cut or tear two rectangles for bib from ¼ yd. cotton fabric. See Cuff Dimensions on page 49. Cut or tear two rectangles for cuffs. See Ruffle Dimensions on page 49. Cut or tear two strips for ruffles. See Waistband Dimensions on page 49. Cut strip for waistband.

2 Using sewing machine, sew front seam from "A" to "C" with right sides together. Sew back seam from "B" to "C."

3 Sew waist and bottom of leg edges with gathering stitch. Pull bobbin thread to gather.

4 Place and pin waistband to gathered waist. Sew in place. Place and pin cuff to gathered leg edge. Sew in place. Fold bottom edge of cuff in ½" and, using iron, press. Topstitch in place.

5 Sew inside leg seam, with right sides together.

6 Fold one long edge of ruffle in ½" and press. Stitch or fuse in place. Repeat with other ruffle. Sew raw edges with gathering stitch. Pull bobbin thread to gather.

7 Fold straps in thirds lengthwise and press. Place and topstitch gathered ruffle to underside edge of strap. Repeat with other ruffle and strap.

8 Sew three sides of bib, with right sides together, leaving bottom edge open. Turn right side out and press. See Illustration #1. Place and pin strap to outside edge of bib. Sew in place. Repeat with remaining strap.

Illustration #1

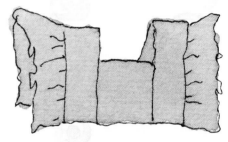

9 Place and pin bib to inside center front waistband of pants. Sew in place. Place and pin back section of strap to inside of waistband. Sew in place. Topstitch around waistband ¼" below bib.

10 Fold back opening in ⅜" and press to hold. Topstitch in place.

11 Using needle and thread, hand-stitch two buttons vertically to one end of waistband. Cut four 6" ribbons. Machine-stitch or hand-stitch two ribbons opposite each button on other end of waistband. Tie ribbons around buttons to secure waist.

Ruffle Dimensions:

12"	8¼" x 2⅜"
14"	9½" x 2⅝"
16"	10¾" x 3"
18"	12" x 3"

Strap Dimensions:

12"	5¾" x 2"
14"	6½" x 2⅜"
16"	7¼" x 2¾"
18"	8" x 3"

Bib Dimensions:

12"	2½" x 2¾"
14"	2¾" x 3"
16"	3" x 3¼"
18"	3¼" x 3½"

Cuff Dimensions:

12"	4½" x 2⅝"
14"	4½" x 2⅝"
16"	5½" x 3"
18"	5½" x 3"

Waistband Dimensions:

12"	7½" x 2"
14"	8½" x 2"
16"	9¾" x 2⅜"
18"	10¾" x 2⅜"

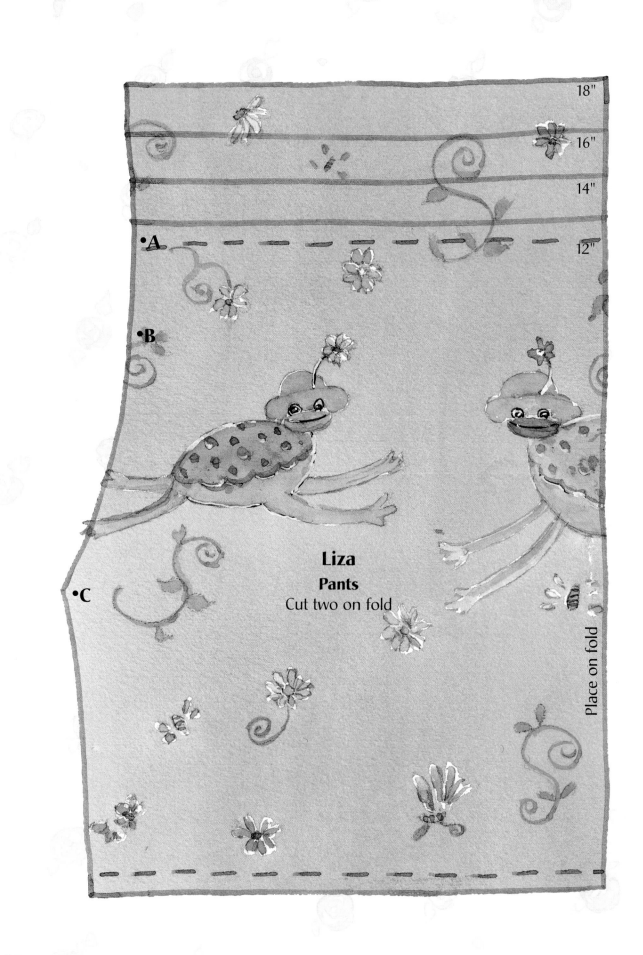

18"

16"

14"

•A

12"

•B

Liza
Pants
Cut two on fold

•C

Place on fold

Hollyhock

Hollyhock

Redesign old or antique petticoats into heirloom dresses. Take advantage of the hand-stitched tucks, antique lace, and trims.

Save precious sewing time by making use of sewn hems and other details. Size and sew a "muslin" dress before cutting into that special petticoat.

Fabric:

Fabric: Antique eyelet lace petticoat
Muslin (½ yd.)

Notions:

Buttons: ⅜" (3)
Fusible hem tape (optional)
Thread

Tools:

Fabric scissors
Iron and ironing board
Measuring tape
Sewing machine
Sewing needle
Straight pins
Tracing paper and pencil

Instructions for Dress

1 Refer to *Essential Basics* on pages 8–15. Using patterns on pages 54–55, trace patterns onto tracing paper. Place and pin patterns to muslin fabric. See Skirt Dimensions on page 55. Cut or tear rectangle for skirt. See Cuff Dimensions on page 55. Using fabric scissors, cut rectangles for cuffs. Cut out pattern pieces. See Bias Dimensions on page 55. Cut rectangle for neck bias. *Optional: See Straight Sleeve Dimensions and Straight Sleeve Cuff Dimensions on page 55. Cut straight sleeve in place of sleeve pattern.*

2 Using needle and thread, baste shoulder seams, with right sides together. Place bodice on doll.

3 Center top of sleeve to shoulder seam and baste in place. Place bodice and sleeve on doll and make any necessary adjustments.

4 Remove bodice from doll and baste side seams in place. Place bodice on doll and make any necessary adjustments.

5 Sew top of skirt with gathering stitch and baste to bodice. Place dress on doll and make any adjustments. *Note: If cutting skirt on finished edge, skirt length may need adjustment.*

6 Remove waistband from petticoat and smooth out fabric.

7 Remove basting stitches, retaining any pattern adjustments. See Illustration #1. Place and pin muslin pattern pieces to petticoat. Using fabric scissors, cut out pattern pieces. *Note: Using existing hem will take advantage of design elements as well as diminish finishing steps.*

8 Using sewing machine, sew shoulder seams, with right sides together. Using iron, press seams open.

9 Sew bias strip to neck edge, with right sides together. Fold bias strip in half to inside of neck edge and machine-stitch or hand-stitch in place. *Optional: Old lace from petticoat may be stitched to neck edge.*

10 Place and pin sleeve onto raw edge of cuff, overlapping ⅜". Sew in place.

11 Sew gathering stitch across top of sleeve across to ease sleeve into armhole. Center and pin top of sleeve to shoulder seam, with right sides together. Sew from center out. Repeat for second sleeve.

Illustration #1

Illustration #2

12 See Illustration #2. Sew side seams of bodice and sleeves, tapering towards wrist, with right sides together. *Note: Be certain that doll's hand can pass through tapered wrist. Straight sleeve will require more tapering than sleeve pattern.*

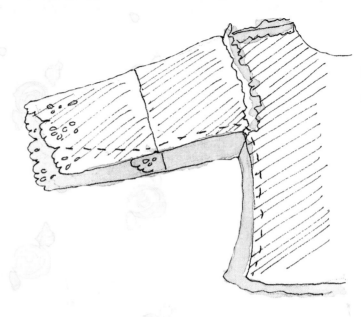

13 Sew top of skirt with two rows of gathering stitches. Pull bobbin threads to gather. Center and pin skirt to bodice, with right sides together. Sew in place.

14 Sew center back edges of skirt, with right sides together, stopping 3" below bodice.

15 Fold center back opening in ⅜" and press. Sew or fuse in place.

16 Hand-stitch one button at back neck edge, midway back bodice, and waist. Cut six 6" ribbons. Machine-stitch or hand-stitch two ribbons opposite buttons on other side of bodice. Tie ribbons around button to secure dress.

17 Pin dress to desired length and press. Machine-stitch, hand-stitch, or fuse in

place. *Note: This step may be eliminated if skirt has been cut out on a finished edge.*

✔ *Two-hour assembly is based on sewing time of finished dress and not on fitting time. This dress will require extra time for fitting.*

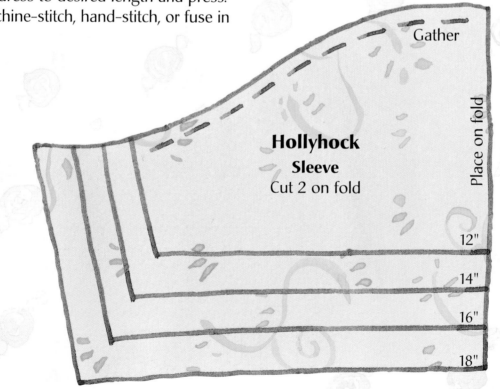

Hollyhock
Sleeve
Cut 2 on fold

Gather

Place on fold

12"
14"
16"
18"

Bias Dimensions:

12"	5¼" x 1¼"
14"	6¼" x 1¼"
16"	8" x 1½"
18"	9½" x 1½"

Skirt Dimensions:

12"	24¼" x 6¾"
14"	28¼" x 7⅝"
16"	32⅛" x 8½"
18"	36" x 9½"

Straight Sleeve Dimensions:

12"	8" x 2½"
14"	8½" x 3⅜"
16"	8" x 1½"
18"	10" x 3¾"

Cuff Dimensions:

12"	7" x 2¼"
14"	7½" x 2⅜"
16"	8" x 2¾"
18"	8¾" x 2⅞"

Straight Sleeve Cuff Dimensions:

12"	8" x 2½"
14"	8½" x 2⅜"
16"	8" x 2¾"
18"	10" x 2⅞"

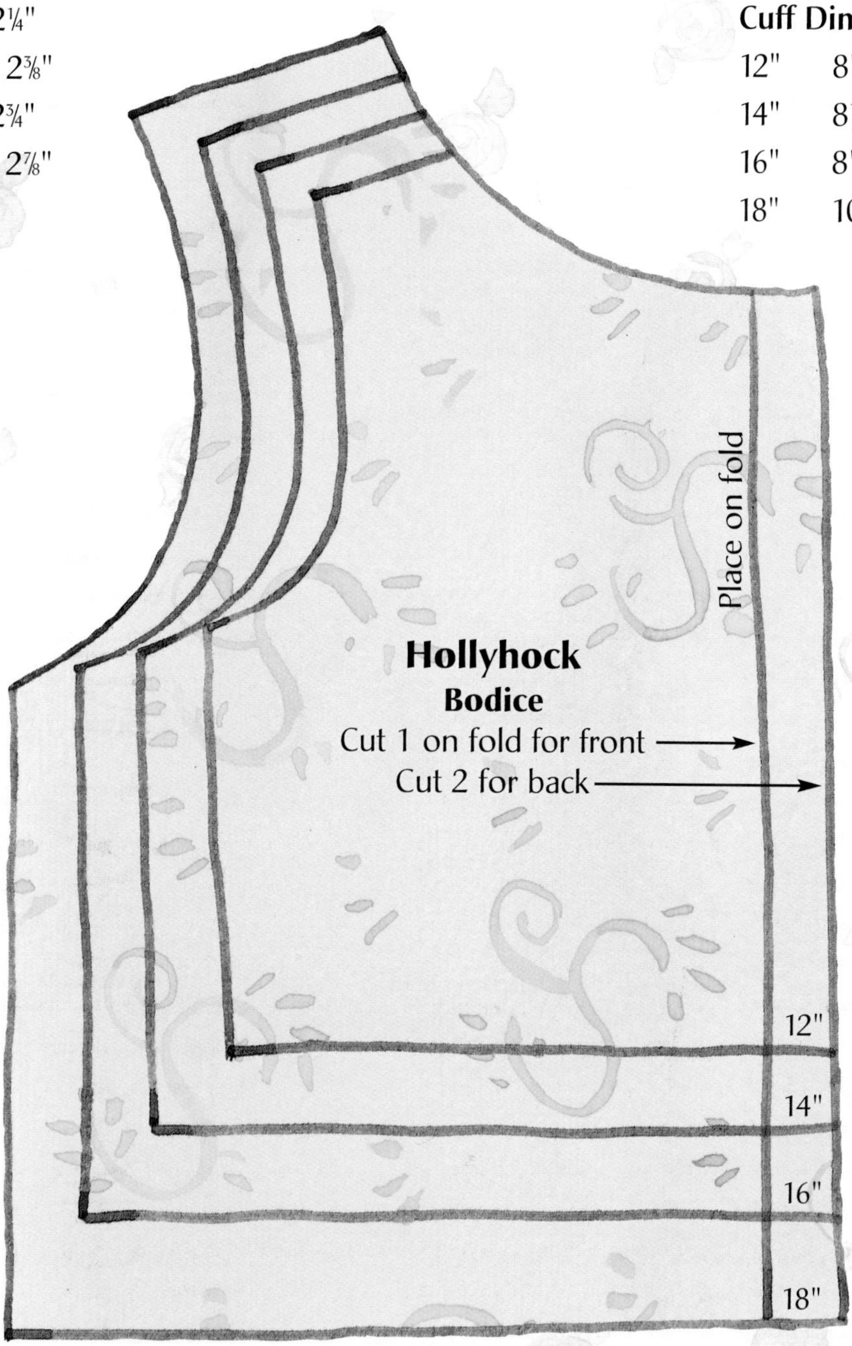

Place on fold

Hollyhock
Bodice
Cut 1 on fold for front →
Cut 2 for back →

12"
14"
16"
18"

chapter 2

Fall Finery

"A" Beatrix and "B" Beatrix

Beatrix

Two adorable variations
originating from the same
pattern, with different trims and
a flounce to create two unique looks.

When this pattern was first designed,
the jacket seemed a little short; so I
added the flounce, and a new style
was created.

Fabric:

Fabric: cotton (½ yd.) (Skirt)
        flannel (¼ yd.) ("A" Duster)
        flannel (½ yd.) ("A" Duster)
        lightweight wool (½ yd.) ("B" Duster)

Notions:

Buttons: ⅜" (1) ("A" Duster)
         1" (4) ("A" Duster)
         ¾" (2) (Skirt)
Fusible hem tape (optional)
Lace: ½"-wide (3 yds.) ("B" Duster)
Thread
Velcro® tabs ("A" Duster)

Tools:

Fabric scissors
Iron and ironing board
Measuring tape
Sewing machine
Sewing needle
Straight pins
Tracing paper and pencil

Instructions for "A" Duster and Skirt

1 Refer to *Essential Basics* on pages 8–15. Using patterns on pages 60–62, trace patterns onto tracing paper. Place and pin duster and sleeve pattern to ½ yd. flannel fabric. See Ruffle Dimensions on page 61. Cut or tear one strip for ruffle. See Interfacing Dimensions on page 62. Using fabric scissors, cut two strips for front interface. Place and pin collar to ¼ yd. flannel fabric. See Cuff Dimensions on page 61. Cut or tear two rectangles for cuffs. See Skirt Dimensions on page 63. Cut rectangle for skirt from cotton fabric. Using measuring tape, determine doll waist circumference, plus 1". Cut 2"-wide strip to these dimensions for waistband. Cut out pattern pieces.

"A" Duster

1 Using sewing machine, sew shoulder seams, with right sides together. Using iron, press seams open.

2 Sew top of sleeve with gathering stitch. Sew wrist end of sleeve with two rows of gathering stitches. Pull all bobbin thread to gather. Repeat for second sleeve

3 Place and pin cuff to wrist end of sleeve, with right sides together. Sew in place. Fold cuff in half to inside of sleeve. Sew or fuse (referring to *NoSew Instructions* on page 15) in place.

4 Center and pin top of sleeve to shoulder seam, with right sides together. Sew sleeve from center out. Repeat for second sleeve.

5 Sew side seams of duster and sleeves, with right sides together. Press seams open.

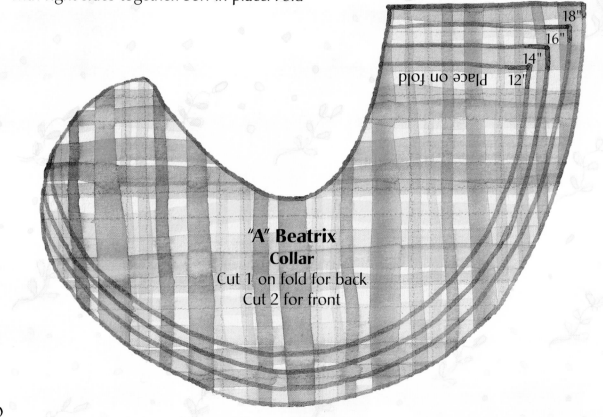

"A" Beatrix
Collar
Cut 1 on fold for back
Cut 2 for front

Place on fold   12"   14"   16"   18"

6 Turn ruffle edge under ⅜" and press. Sew or fuse in place.

7 Sew long raw edge of ruffle with gathering stitch. Pull bobbin thread to gather.

8 Place and pin gathered ruffle to bottom edge of duster, with right sides together. Sew in place.

9 Sew interface to center front edge, with right sides together. Turn right side out and sew or fuse in place.

10 Sew outside edge of collar, with right sides together. Turn right side out and press flat.

11 Center and pin collar to neck edge, with right sides together. Sew in place.

12 Using needle and thread, hand-stitch four 1" buttons to front of duster. Hand-stitch two ¾" buttons to outside of each cuff. Attach Velcro tabs to top of neckline for closure.

Cuff Dimensions:

12"	4½" x 1¾"
14"	5⅛" x 1¾"
16"	5¾" x 2"
18"	6¼" x 2"

Ruffle Dimensions:

12"	19" x 2"
14"	22" x 2"
16"	25" x 2½"
18"	28" x 2½"

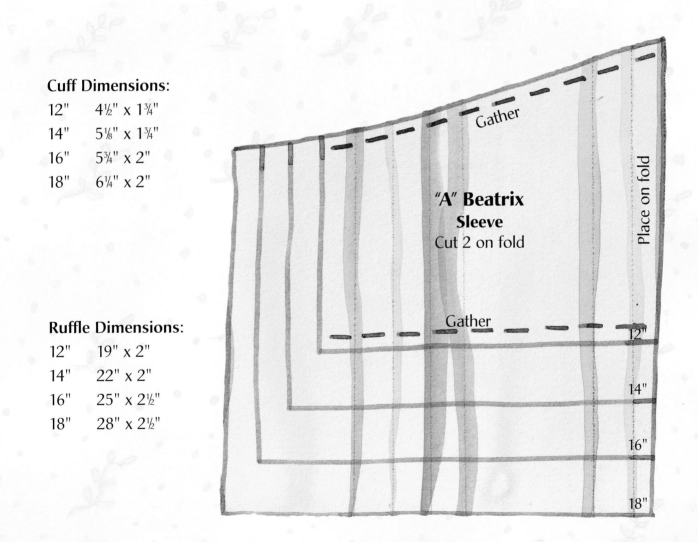

"A" Beatrix Sleeve
Cut 2 on fold

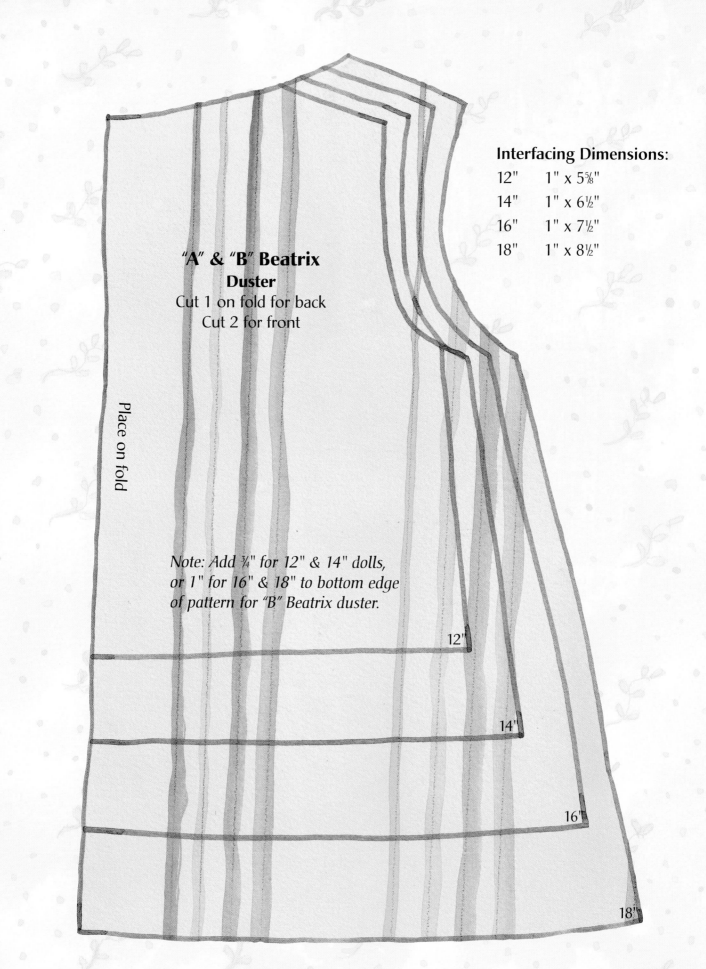

Interfacing Dimensions:

Size	Dimensions
12"	1" x 5⅝"
14"	1" x 6½"
16"	1" x 7½"
18"	1" x 8½"

"A" & "B" Beatrix
Duster
Cut 1 on fold for back
Cut 2 for front

Place on fold

Note: Add ¾" for 12" & 14" dolls, or 1" for 16" & 18" to bottom edge of pattern for "B" Beatrix duster.

12"

14"

16"

18"

Skirt

1 See Tuck Chart below. Using iron, press first tuck below top edge of skirt piece, following Tuck Chart. Using straight pins, pin tuck ½" from fold and press. Using sewing machine, sew tuck in place. Press second tuck below first tuck and press. Pin and sew in place. Turn hem under 1" and press. Sew or fuse (referring to *NoSew Instructions* on page 15) in place.

2 Sew top of skirt with two rows of gathering stitches. Pull bobbin threads to gather.

3 Place and pin waistband to gathered waist. Sew in place. Fold waistband in half to inside of skirt, tucking the waistband ends inside, and press. Sew or fuse in place.

4 Sew back seam of skirt, with right sides together, stopping 2" below waist. Fold opening of skirt and waistband in ⅜" and press. Machine-stitch, hand-stitch, or fuse in place.

5 Using needle and thread, hand-stitch ⅜" button to one end of waistband. Sew two 6" ribbons to opposite end of waistband. Tie ribbons around button to secure waist.

6 Turn edge of skirt under to desired length. Machine-stitch, hand-stitch, or fuse in place.

Skirt Dimensions:

12"	16¼" x 9⅞"
14"	18⅞" x 11"
16"	21½" x 12⅛"
18"	24" x 13⅛"

Tuck Chart

	12"	14"	16"	18"
1st tuck	4⅝"	5½"	6¼"	7"
2nd tuck	1"	1¼"	1½"	2"

"B" Duster

1 Refer to *Essential Basics* on pages 8–15. Using patterns on pages 62 and 64, trace patterns onto tracing paper. Place and pin duster and sleeve pattern to wool fabric. See Interfacing Dimensions on page 62. Using fabric scissors, cut two strips for front interface. See Bias Dimensions on page 64. Cut bias strip for collar. Cut out pattern pieces.

2 Using sewing machine, sew shoulder seams with right sides together. Using iron, press seams open.

3 Sew top of sleeve with gathering stitch. Pull bobbin thread to gather.

4 Center and pin sleeve to shoulder seam, with right sides together. Sew sleeve from center out. Repeat for second sleeve.

5 Fold wrist end of sleeve in ⅜" and sew or fuse (referring to *NoSew Instructions* on page 15) in place. Sew lace to sleeves ⅜" from wrist edge.

6 Sew side seams of duster and sleeves, with right sides together. Press seams open. Sew interface to center front edge, with right sides together. Turn right side out and sew or fuse in place.

7 Turn bottom edge of duster under to desired length and press. Sew or fuse in place.

8 Sew lace around hem edge. Sew second row of lace 1¼" above duster hem.

9 Sew collar bias to neck edge, with right sides together. Fold bias strip in half to inside of collar and sew in place.

10 Cut 32" piece of lace. Center and pin lace to inside of collar, leaving equal lengths of lace unattached. Sew lace in place. Use unattached lace to tie as closure.

✔ *"B" Duster is worn over Hollyhock dress shown on pages 51-55.*

Bias Dimensions:

12"	7" x 1½"
14"	9" x 1½"
16"	11¾" x 2"
18"	12½" x 2"

Gather

"B" Beatrix
Sleeve
Cut 2 on fold

Place on fold

12"

14"

16"

18"

Ellen

Ellen

This heirloom-style teadress was made with beautiful antique lace and ribbon embellishments applied to a pastel plaid cotton fabric.

Fabric:

Fabric: cotton (¾ yd.)

Notions:

Elastic: ⅜"-wide (⅛ yd.) (optional)
Fabric glue
Fusible hem tape
Lace: antique medallion
      1"-wide (½ yd.)
      1½"-wide (2 yds.)
Ribbon: ¾"-wide decorative (1¼ yds.)
        ⅜"-wide grosgrain (½ yd.) (optional)
Thread
Velcro® tabs

Tools:

Fabric scissors
Iron and ironing board
Measuring tape
Sewing machine
Sewing needle
Straight pins
Tracing paper and pencil

Instructions for Teadress

1 Refer to *Essential Basics* on pages 8–15. Using patterns on pages 67–69, trace patterns onto tracing paper. Place and pin pattern to cotton fabric. Using fabric scissors, cut out fabric pattern pieces. See Skirt Dimensions below. Cut or tear rectangle for skirt.

2 Using sewing machine, sew shoulder seams, with right sides together. Using iron, press seams open.

3 Fold neck edge in ¼" and press. Sew 1"-wide lace to inside of neck edge with either zigzag or straight stitch.

4 Cut two 6" pieces of 1½"-wide lace. Fit wrist end of sleeve to lace and pin in place over right side of fabric. Sew lace to sleeve with zigzag stitch. Repeat for second sleeve.

5 See Illustration #1. Make tucks by turning wrist end of sleeve under 1½" and press. Sew entire width of sleeve ¼" from fold. Make second tuck 1" above first tuck. Repeat for second sleeve.

Illustration #1

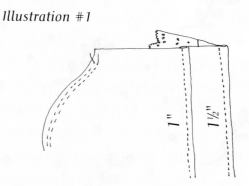

Skirt Dimensions:

12"	14" x 8"
14"	16" x 9¼"
16"	18" x 10½"
18"	20" x 11⅝"

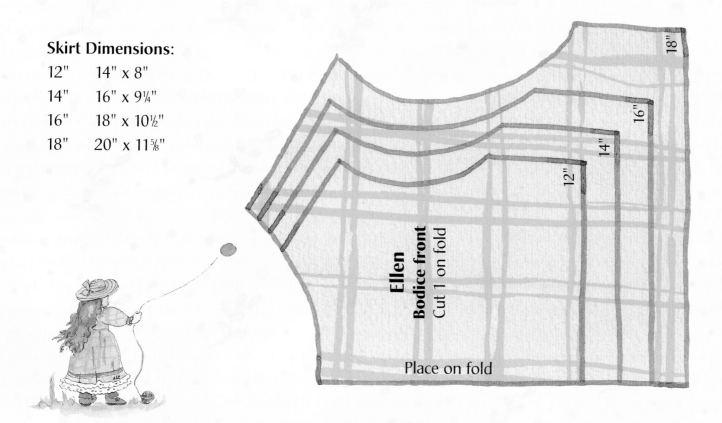

Ellen
Bodice front
Cut 1 on fold

Place on fold

6 Sew top of sleeve with gathering stitch. Sew wrist end of sleeve with two rows of gathering stitches. Pull all bobbin threads to gather each sleeve end.

7 *Optional: Wrist end of sleeve may be gathered by sewing 5" of ⅜" elastic to inside of sleeve above lace; or 9" piece of grosgrain ribbon may be tied around sleeve after completion of dress.*

8 Center and pin gathered sleeve to shoulder seam, with right sides together. Sew sleeve from center out. Repeat for second sleeve. *Optional: Sleeve may be basted in place if desired.*

9 Sew side seams of bodice and sleeves, with right sides together. Press seams open.

10 Turn skirt hem under 2" and press. Refer to *NoSew Instructions* on page 15. Using iron, fuse hem with fusible hem tape. Using fabric glue, bond 1½"-wide lace to underside of hem, allowing 1" of lace to hang below hemline.

11 Using fabric glue, bond decorative ribbon 3" above bottom edge of skirt.

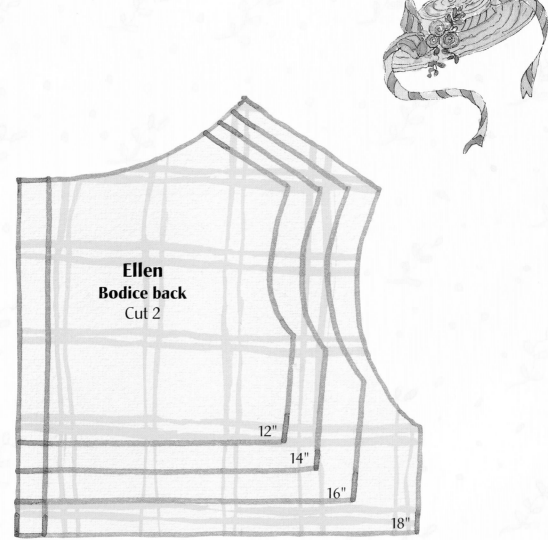

Ellen
Bodice back
Cut 2

12"

14"

16"

18"

12 Sew top of skirt with two rows of gathering stitches. Pull bobbin threads to gather. Center and pin skirt to bodice, with right sides together. Sew in place.

13 Sew center back edges of skirt, with right sides together, stopping 2" below bodice.

14 Fold center back opening in ⅜" and press. Sew or fuse in place. Attach Velcro tabs for closures.

15 Using needle and thread, tack lace medallion to bodice front.

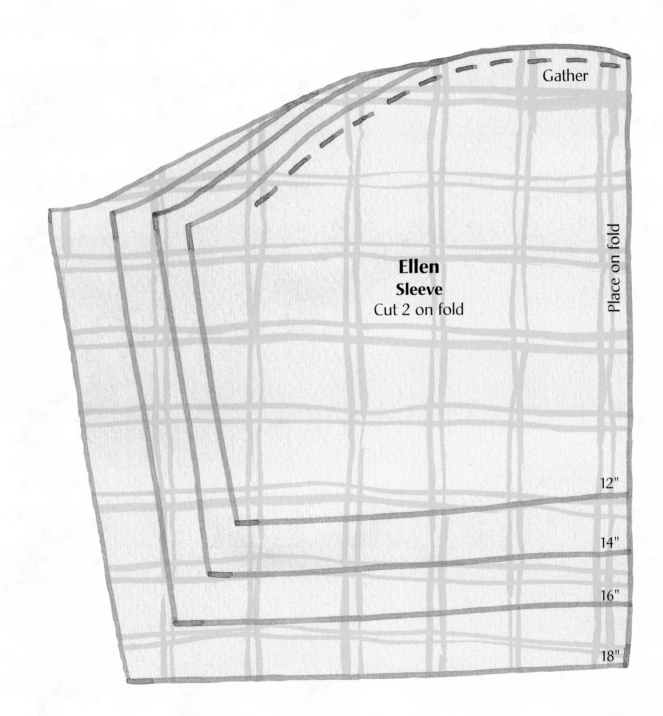

Gather

Place on fold

Ellen
Sleeve
Cut 2 on fold

12"

14"

16"

18"

Whitney

Whitney

Hearts and a bow set off this lovely party dress of gold, sprinkled with polka dots. Add the perfect accessory, such as a pretty straw hat, and Whitney is ready to attend the party with her little mouse friend.

Fabric:

Fabric: cotton (¼ yd.)
       cotton (⅓ yd.)

Notions:

Buttons: ⅜" (5)
Fusible bond paper
Fusible hem tape
Lace: ⅜"-wide (½ yd.)
      ⅝"-wide (1 yd.)
Ribbon: ⅜"-wide satin (1 yd.)
        ⅝"-wide satin (1 yd.)
Thread
Velcro® tabs

Tools:

Embroidery needle
Fabric scissors
Iron and ironing board
Measuring tape
Sewing needle
Sewing machine (optional)
Straight pins
Tracing paper and pencil

Instructions for Dress

1 Refer to *Essential Basics* on pages 8–15. Using patterns on pages 72–74, trace patterns onto tracing paper. Place and pin dress patterns to ⅓ yd. cotton fabric. See Skirt Dimensions on page 73. Cut or tear one rectangle for skirt. See Cuff Dimensions on page 73. Using fabric scissors, cut two rectangles for cuffs. Cut out pattern pieces.

2 Place and pin ⅜"-wide ribbon vertically 1¾" from center front on each side of bodice front. Using sewing machine, sew in place. Place and pin ribbon horizontally ¾" from bottom edge. Sew in place. Place and pin ribbon horizontally ¾" below neck edge. Sew in place.

3 Trace one bow and five heart patterns onto paper side of fusible webbing. Cut square around bow and hearts. Using iron, fuse bow and hearts to ¼ yd. fabric.

4 Cut out bow and heart motifs and remove paper backing. Place bow and hearts as desired on bodice front and fuse. Using embroidery needle and embroidery floss, embroider stems onto bodice. *Optional: Quilt around hearts with embroidery floss for accent.*

5 Sew shoulder seams, with right sides together. Using iron, press seams open.

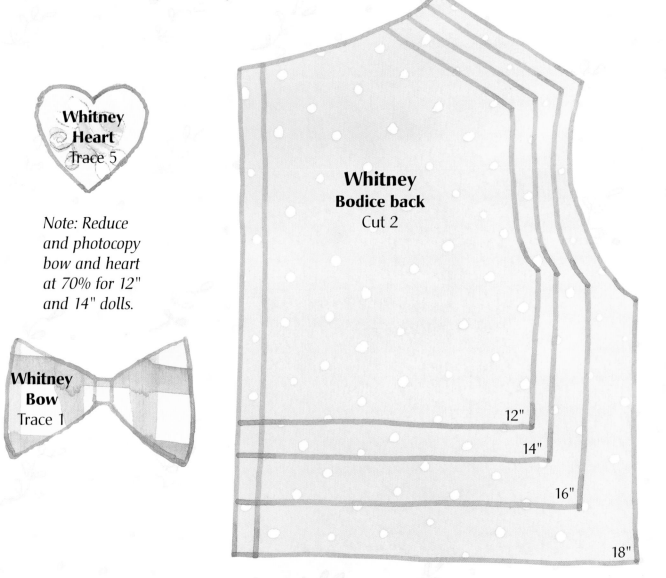

Whitney Heart
Trace 5

Note: Reduce and photocopy bow and heart at 70% for 12" and 14" dolls.

Whitney Bow
Trace 1

Whitney Bodice back
Cut 2

12"

14"

16"

18"

6 Fold neck edge in ¼" and press. Sew or fuse (referring to *NoSew Instructions* on page 15) with fusible hem tape. Sew ⅜"-wide lace to inside of neck edge.

7 Sew wrist end of sleeve with gathering stitch. Pull bobbin thread to gather. Place and pin sleeve cuff to wrist end of sleeve, with right sides together. Sew in place. Fold cuff in half and press. Sew in place.

8 Sew top of sleeve with gathering stitch. Pull bobbin thread to gather. Center and pin top of sleeve to shoulder seam, with right sides together. Sew from center out. Repeat for second sleeve.

9 Sew side seams of bodice and sleeves, with right sides together.

Cuff Dimensions:

12"	2¾" x 1"
14"	3" x 1¼"
16"	3⅜" x 1¼"
18"	3⅝" x 1¼"

Skirt Dimensions:

12"	24⅜" x 4¾"
14"	28¼" x 6"
16"	32" x 7¼"
18"	36" x 8½"

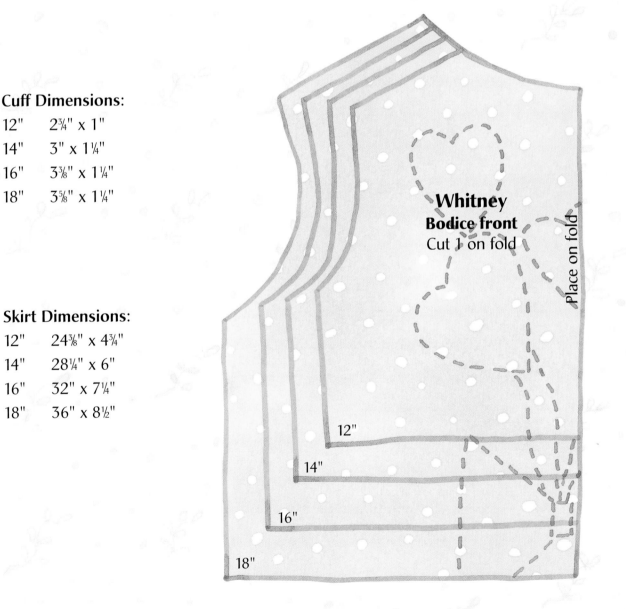

Whitney
Bodice front
Cut 1 on fold

Place on fold

12"
14"
16"
18"

10 Sew one long edge of skirt with gathering stitch. Pull bobbin thread to gather.

11 Turn hem under to desired length and press. Sew or fuse in place. Sew ⅝"-wide lace to underside of hem. Sew ⅝"-wide ribbon ¼" above hem, allowing lace to extend below hemline.

12 Center and pin gathered skirt to bodice, with right sides together. Sew in place.

13 Sew center back edges of skirt, with right sides together, stopping 2" below bodice.

14 Fold center back opening in ⅜" and press. Sew or fuse in place. Attach Velcro tabs for closures. Using sewing needle and thread, hand-stitch five buttons to back for embellishment.

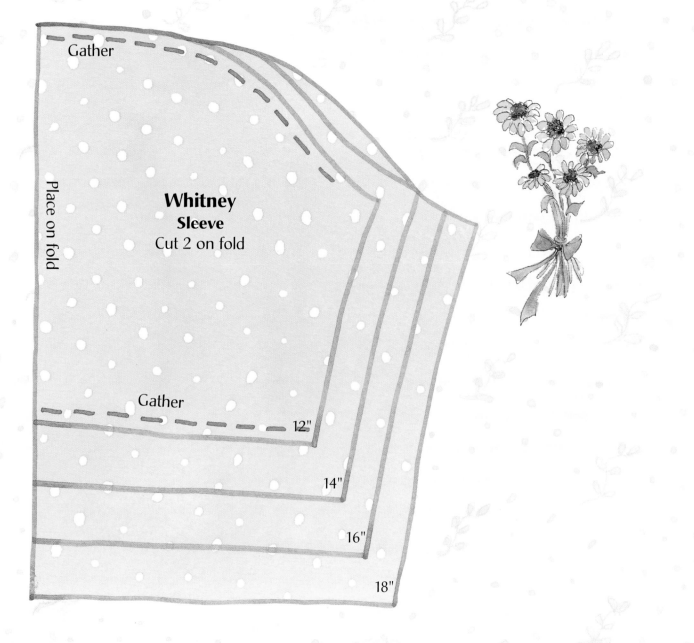

Gather

Place on fold

Whitney
Sleeve
Cut 2 on fold

Gather

12"

14"

16"

18"

Miss Dottie and Rachael

Miss Dottie

This blouse and jumper are great for a mother-daughter project, since they are sewn by hand. This is the perfect opportunity to teach basic sewing stitches and assembly. Think of this as the beginning for creating a "keepsake" garment.

Fabric:

Fabric: cotton (¼ yd.)
        cotton (⅓ yd.)

Notions:

Buttons: ½" decorative (3)
Fusible hem tape
Lace: ¾"-wide (½ yd.)
     1"-wide (1 yd.)
     2"-wide double-sided (6")
Ribbon: ⅛"-wide satin (⅓ yd.)
Thread
Velcro® tabs

Tools:

Fabric scissors
Iron and ironing board
Measuring tape
Sewing needle
Sewing machine (optional)
Straight pins
Tracing paper and pencil

Instructions for Blouse and Jumper

1 Refer to *Essential Basics* on pages 8–15. Using patterns on pages 78–79, trace patterns onto tracing paper. See Bib Dimensions on page 80. Cut or tear bib from ⅓ yd. cotton fabric. See Skirt Dimensions on page 80. Cut or tear rectangle for skirt. See Strap Dimensions on page 80. Cut or tear two rectangles for straps. Cut or tear one 2½" x doll waist circumference, plus 1" strip for waistband. Place and pin blouse pattern to ¼ yd. cotton fabric. See Cuff Dimensions below. Cut or tear two strips for cuffs. See Bias Dimensions below. Cut bias strip for neck. Using fabric scissors, cut out pattern pieces.

Blouse

1 Using needle and thread, hand-stitch (5–6 stitches per inch) shoulder seams, with right sides together. *Optional: Sewing machine may be used for sewing, if desired.* Using iron, press seams open.

2 Refer to *Stitch Guide* on page 14. Hand-stitch top and wrist end of sleeve, with gathering stitch. Gather top and bottom edges.

3 Place and pin wrist end of sleeve to cuff edge, with right sides together. Hand-stitch in place. Fold cuff in half to inside of sleeve and stitch in place. Hand-stitch ¾"-wide lace to inside of wrist band. Repeat for second sleeve.

4 Gather, center, and pin top of sleeve to shoulder seam, with right sides together. Hand-stitch from center out. Repeat for second sleeve.

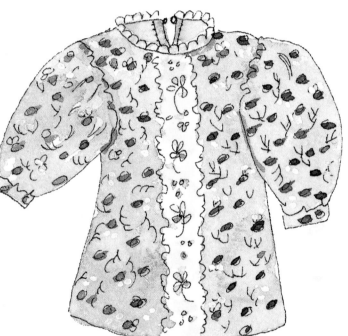

Bias Dimensions:

12"	6" x ¾"
14"	6⅞" x ¾"
16"	7¾" x ¾"
18"	8½" x ¾"

Cuff Dimensions:

12"	2⅜" x 1¼"
14"	2⅝" x 1¼"
16"	2⅞" x 1⅜"
18"	3⅛" x 1⅜"

5 Center and pin 2"-wide lace to front bodice and hand-stitch in place. Hand-stitch bias strip to neck edge, with right sides together.

6 Fold bias strip in half to inside of neck edge, and hand-stitch in place with overcast stitch. Hand-stitch ¾"-wide lace to inside of neck edge.

7 Hand-stitch side seams, with right sides together. Press seams open. Turn bottom edge of blouse under and press. Hand-stitch in place with running stitch.

8 Fold back opening to inside of blouse and press. Hand-stitch in place. Attach Velcro tabs for closures.

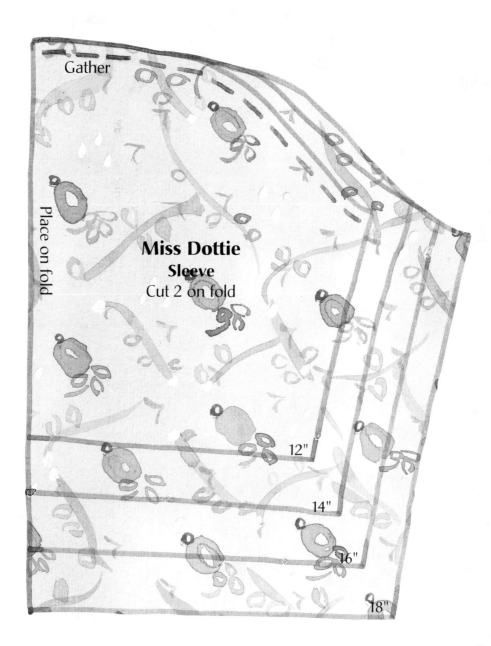

Gather

Place on fold

Miss Dottie
Sleeve
Cut 2 on fold

12"

14"

16"

18"

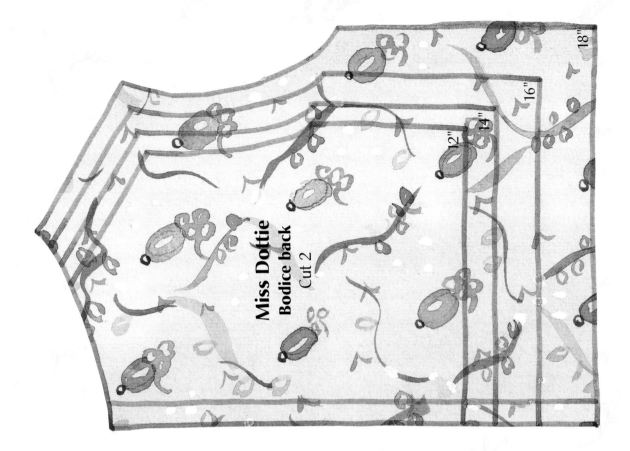

Miss Dottie
Bodice back
Cut 2

12"
14"
16"
18"

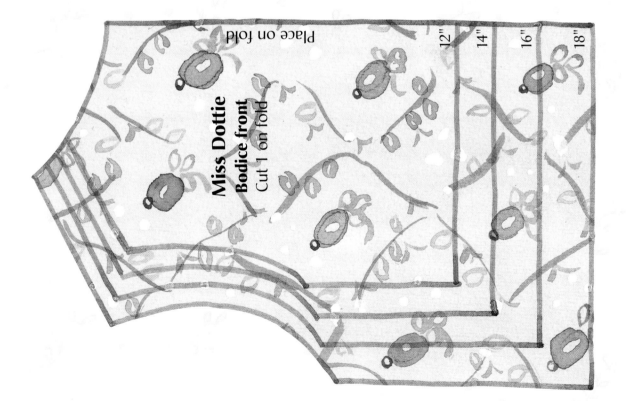

Place on fold

Miss Dottie
Bodice front
Cut 1 on fold

12"
14"
16"
18"

Jumper

1 Refer to *Stitch Guide* on page 14. See Illustration #1. Using needle and thread, hand-stitch (5–6 stitches per inch) one long side of skirt with gathering stitch. *Optional: Sewing machine may be used for sewing, if desired.*

2 Gather and pin skirt to waistband, with right sides together, leaving ½" seam allowance at each end. Hand-stitch in place. Fold waistband in ⅛" and press. Fold waistband in half to inside of skirt, and hand-stitch in place with overcast stitch.

3 Turn bottom edge of skirt under ⅛" and press. Turn bottom edge under 1" again, and press. Hand-stitch in place.

4 Hand-stitch sides of folded bib, with right sides together. Turn right side out. Using iron, press flat. Turn bottom raw edges under ⅛" and press. Center and pin bib to front center of waistband. Hand-stitch in place.

5 Fold strap pieces in thirds widthwise, turning raw edge under ⅛" and press. Hand-stitch sides of straps with running stitch. Place and pin straps to front of bib. Hand-stitch in place.

6 Hand-stitch skirt back seam, with right sides together, stopping 4" below waist. Fold back opening in ⅜" and press. Hand-stitch in place.

Illustration #1

7 Place skirt on doll and adjust straps to back of skirt. Place and pin straps to back of skirt. Remove skirt and hand-stitch straps in place.

8 Hand-stitch button to one end of waistband. Hand-stitch two 6" ribbons to opposite end of waistband. Tie ribbons around button to secure waist.

9 Hand-stitch two buttons to bottom outside edges of bib for decoration.

Bib Dimensions:		Skirt Dimensions:		Strap Dimensions:	
12"	2⅛" x 2½"	12"	20¼" x 6¾"	12"	5¾" x 1"
14"	2¼" x 2¾"	14"	23½" x 7¾"	14"	6½" x 1"
16"	2½" x 3"	16"	26¾" x 8¾"	16"	7¼" x 1¼"
18"	2¾" x 3¼"	18"	30" x 9½"	18"	8" x 1¼"

Rachael

A hint of Southwest influence is introduced with this outfit. The charming vest is sewn from a crushed velvet with an antique ribbon trim. The skirt is three-tiered and adorable on this antique doll.

Fabric:

Fabric: cotton (⅓ yd.)
crushed velvet (¼ yd.)

Notions:

Buttons ⅜" (3) (optional)
Fray preventative
Fusible hem tape
Ribbon: ¼"-wide embroidered (1yd.)
Thread
Velcro® tabs

Tools:

Fabric scissors
Iron and ironing board
Measuring tape
Sewing machine
Sewing needle
Straight pins
Tracing paper and pencil

Instructions for Dress and Vest

1 Refer to *Essential Basics* on pages 8–15. Using patterns on pages 82 and 84, trace patterns onto tracing paper. Place and pin vest pattern to crushed velvet fabric. Place and pin dress pattern to cotton fabric. Using fabric scissors, cut out pattern pieces. See Strip #1, #2, and #3 Dimensions below. Cut or tear one strip for each from cotton fabric for skirt.

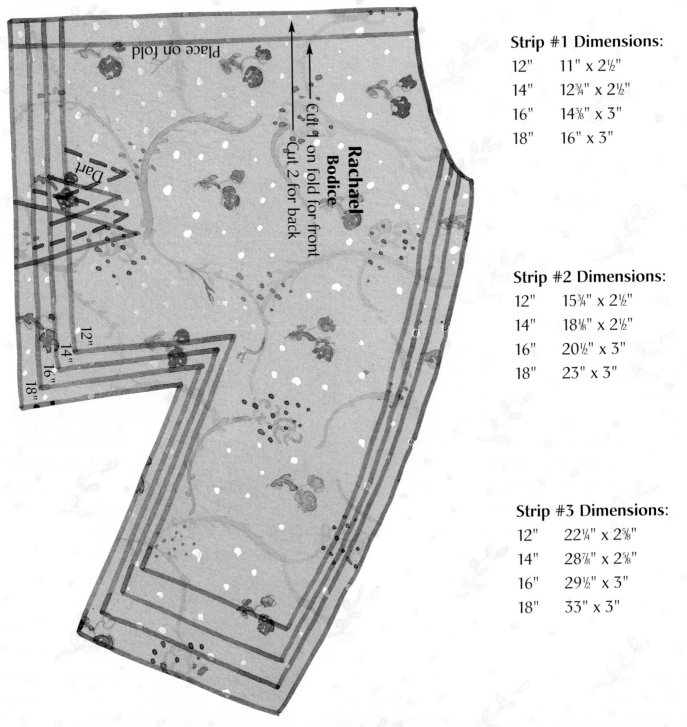

Place on fold

Dart

Cut 1 on fold for front
Cut 2 for back

Rachael Bodice

12"
14"
16"
18"

Strip #1 Dimensions:

12"	11" x 2½"
14"	12¾" x 2½"
16"	14⅜" x 3"
18"	16" x 3"

Strip #2 Dimensions:

12"	15¾" x 2½"
14"	18⅛" x 2½"
16"	20½" x 3"
18"	23" x 3"

Strip #3 Dimensions:

12"	22¼" x 2⅝"
14"	28⅞" x 2⅝"
16"	29½" x 3"
18"	33" x 3"

Dress

1 Using sewing machine, sew ⅛" seam down front bodice pieces, with right sides together. Mark darts and sew in place.

2 Sew shoulder and upper sleeve seams, with right sides together. Using iron, press seams open.

3 Fold neck edge in ⅛" and press. Machine-stitch or hand-stitch in place. Repeat with wrist end of sleeve.

4 Sew bodice and lower sleeve seams, with right sides together. Press seams open.

5 Sew one long edge of each fabric strip with two rows of gathering stitches or hand-stitch one row of tiny stitches (six stitches per inch) and gather.

6 Pin and sew ungathered side of #1 strip to gathered side of #2 strip. Pin and sew ungathered side of #2 strip to gathered side of #3 strip. Fold ungathered #3 strip edge in ⅛" and press. Machine-stitch, hand-stitch, or fuse (referring to *NoSew Instructions* on page 15) in place.

7 Place and pin gathered skirt to bodice waist, with right sides together. Sew in place.

8 Sew center back edges of dress, with right sides together, stopping 1" below waist.

9 Fold center back opening in ⅜" and press. Sew or fuse in place. Attach Velcro tabs for closures.

Vest

1 Using sewing machine, sew shoulder seams with, right sides together. Using iron, press seams open.

2 Using needle and thread, topstitch arm openings, using small stitches. Place a small amount of fray preventative on edge of arm openings, following manufacturer's instructions. Test on scrap piece of fabric first.

Note: Fray preventative may not be necessary if velour is used.

3 Sew side seams, with right sides together. Press seams open. Topstitch around neck, front, and bottom of vest. Sew ribbon around neck, front, and bottom of vest. *Optional: Hand-stitch buttons to front of vest.*

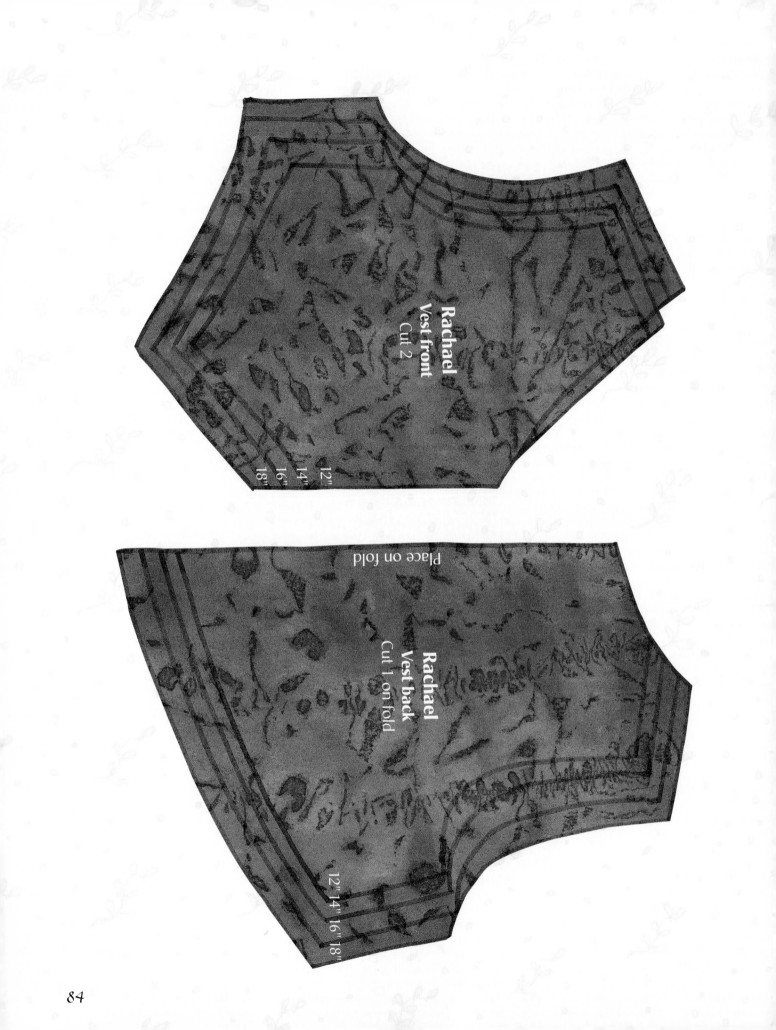

Rachael
Vest front
Cut 2

12"
14"
16"
18"

Place on fold

Rachael
Vest back
Cut 1 on fold

12" 14" 16" 18"

Phoebe

Phoebe

Coveralls are so cute on little children, so why not for dolls? Gingham table napkins were used for the coveralls. Old discarded blue jeans also could be used.

Two contrasting and patterned fabrics make up the shirt, which gives this ensemble a charming country look.

Fabric:

Fabric: cotton (scrap)
        cotton (¼ yd.)
        cotton (⅓ yd.)

Notions:

Embroidery floss
Fusible hem tape
Hook and eye (1)
Novelty buttons (2)
Thread
Velcro® tabs

Tools:

Fabric scissors
Iron and ironing board
Measuring tape
Sewing needle
Sewing machine
Straight pins
Tracing paper and pencil

Instructions for Shirt and Coveralls

1 Refer to *Essential Basics* on pages 8–15. Using patterns on pages 88–89, trace patterns onto tracing paper. Place and pin coverall pattern to ⅓ yd. cotton fabric. See Waistband Dimensions below. Cut or tear one strip for waistband. See Strap Dimensions below. Using fabric scissors, cut two strips for straps. See Bib Dimensions below. Cut or tear two squares for bib. See Pocket Dimensions below. Cut or tear one rectangle for bib pocket. Place and pin shirt pattern to ¼ yd. cotton fabric. See Bias Dimensions below. Cut bias strip for neck edge from scrap fabric. See Cuff Dimensions below. Cut two strips for sleeve cuff. Cut out pattern pieces.

Shirt

1 Using sewing machine, sew shoulder and upper sleeve seams, with right sides together. Using iron, press seams open.

2 Sew bias strip to neck edge, with right sides together. Fold bias strip in half to inside of neck edge and machine-stitch or hand-stitch in place.

3 Fold back edges of shirt in ⅜" and press. Machine-stitch, hand-stitch, or fuse, (referring to *NoSew Instructions* on page 15) with hem tape in place.

4 Sew cuff strip to wrist end of sleeve, with right sides together. Fold cuff piece to inside of sleeve. Machine-stitch, hand-stitch, or fuse in place. Repeat for second sleeve.

5 Sew side and lower sleeve seams, with right sides together. Press seams open.

6 Attach Velcro tabs for closures.

Bias Dimensions:		Bib Dimensions:		Cuff Dimensions:		Pocket Dimensions:	
12"	6¼" x 1¼"	12"	2¾" x 2¾"	12"	4½" x 1½"	12"	2½" x 3"
14"	7¼" x 1¼"	14"	3¼" x 3¼"	14"	4⅞" x 1¾"	14"	2¼" x 2¾"
16"	8⅛" x 1¼"	16"	3⅝" x 3⅝"	16"	5½" x 1⅞"	16"	2" x 2½"
18"	9" x 1¼"	18"	4" x 4"	18"	6" x 2"	18"	1¾" x 2¼"

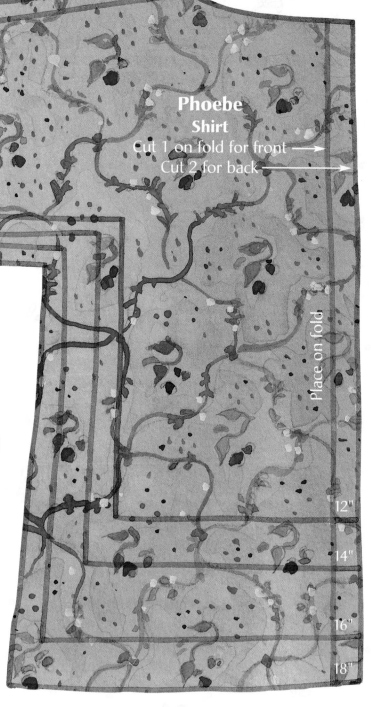

Phoebe
Shirt
Cut 1 on fold for front →
Cut 2 for back ————→

Place on fold

12"

14"

16"

18"

Coveralls

1 Using sewing machine, sew front seam from "A" to "C," with right sides together. Mark pleats and fold. Sew across folded pleat at waistline.

2 Fold leg bottoms in at hemline and, using iron, press. Topstitch leg hem with two rows of stitches, ¼" and 1" from hem edge.

3 Place and pin waistband to pants. Sew in place. Fold waistband in half to inside of coveralls. Topstitch in place.

4 Sew ⅛" seam allowance on three sides of bib pieces, with right sides together. Turn right side out and topstitch same three sides.

5 Fold all edges in ⅛" on pocket and press. Center and pin pocket on bib. Topstitch pocket to bib, leaving top open. Topstitch up the middle of pocket dividing pocket in two.

6 Fold strap pieces in thirds and press. Using iron, fuse (referring to *NoSew Instructions*
on page 15) in place with hem tape. Topstitch ⅛" from edge on both sides of straps. Place and pin straps to bib. Topstitch ¼" from edge around top and sides of bib.

7 Center and pin bib to front center of waistband. Topstitch in place.

8 Sew back seam from "B" to "C" with right sides together. Sew inside leg seam with right sides together.

9 Fold back opening in ⅛" and press. Topstitch or fuse in place. Sew hook and eye to waistband for closure.

10 Place coveralls on doll and pin straps to back of waistband. Remove coveralls and sew straps in place.

11 Using needle and embroidery floss, hand-stitch decorative buttons to front of bib, tying knot on top of button. Trim floss ½" from knot.

Strap Dimensions:

12"	7¼" x 1¾"
14"	8¾" x 2"
16"	9½" x 2¼"
18"	10½" x 2½"

Waistband Dimensions:

12"	7¾" x 2"
14"	9" x 2⅛"
16"	10¼" x 2¼"
18"	11½" x 2½"

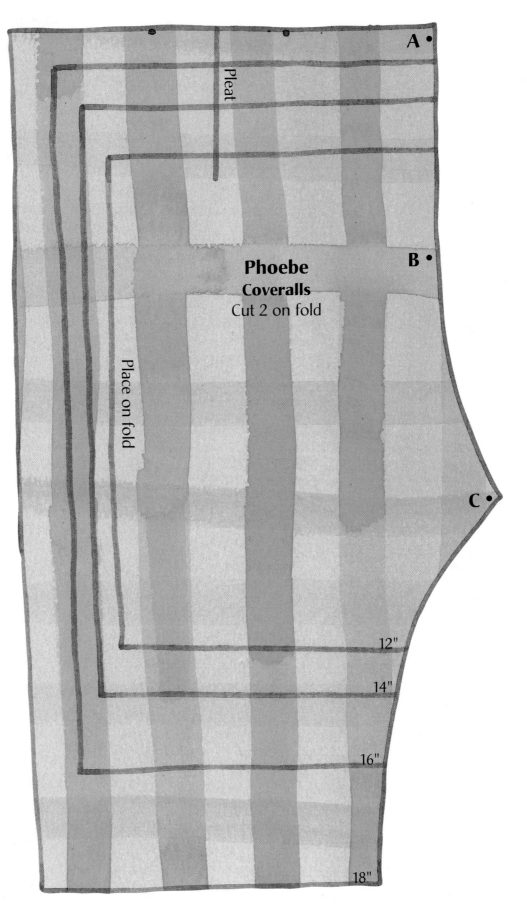

Pleat

A •

B •

Phoebe
Coveralls
Cut 2 on fold

Place on fold

C •

12"

14"

16"

18"

Alice

Alice

Sew an adorable pinafore from strips of fabric that are measured and torn or cut to size. If a more rustic look is desired, ruffle may be left with a torn edge. Pinking scissors give a sawtooth edge.

Fabric:
Fabric: cotton (¾ yd.)

Notions:
Fusible hem tape (optional)
Ribbon: 1"-wide satin (⅔ yd.)
        ¼"-wide (⅔ yd.)
Thread

Tools:
Fabric scissors
Iron and ironing board
Measuring tape
Sewing machine
Straight pins
Tracing paper and pencil

Instructions for Pinafore

1 Refer to *Essential Basics* on pages 8–15. Using pattern on page 93, trace pattern onto tracing paper. Place and pin bib pattern to cotton fabric. Using fabric scissors, cut out pattern pieces. See Skirt Dimensions below. Cut or tear rectangle for skirt. See Skirt Ruffle Dimensions below. Cut or tear four strips for skirt ruffles. See Waistband Dimensions below. Cut or tear strip for waistband. See Sleeve Ruffle Dimensions below. Cut or tear two strips for strap ruffles.

2 Using sewing machine, sew top and sides of bib pieces, with right sides together. Turn right side out and press.

3 Sew short ends of two 4" skirt strips together to form one. Repeat with remaining skirt strips. Fold long edges of all ruffle pieces in ½" and, using iron, press. Sew or fuse (referring to *NoSew Instructions* on page 15) edge with hem tape. Repeat with bottom of skirt piece. *Note: Ruffle edges may be left raw, if desired.* Fold sides of skirt in ½" and press. Sew or fuse in place.

4 Sew top of skirt and one long edge of ruffles with two rows of gathering stitches. Pull bobbin threads to gather.

Skirt Dimensions:

12"	20¼" x 6⅝"
14"	23½" x 7½"
16"	26¾" x 8½"
18"	30" x 9⅜"

Sleeve Ruffle Dimensions:

12"	1¾" x 11"
14"	1¾" x 1½"
16"	2" x 14¼"
18"	2" x 16"

Skirt Ruffle Dimensions:

12"	30" x 3"
14"	34¾" x 3⅜"
16"	39¾" x 3¾"
18"	44" x 4"

Waistband Dimensions:

12"	7⅜" x 1½"
14"	8¾" x 1½"
16"	9⅞" x 1¾"
18"	11" x 1¾"

5 Sew three sides of waistband pieces, with right sides together. Turn right side out, fold in raw edges and sew.

6 Place and pin gathered skirt ruffle to bottom of skirt, matching ruffle hem to skirt hem. Sew in place with two rows of stitches. *Note: If longer pinafore is desired, sew bottom ruffle to fall below hemline.*

7 Place and pin second gathered skirt ruffle to overlap top of first ruffle. Sew in place.

8 Place and pin gathered skirt to waistband. Sew in place, using ¼" seam allowance.

9 Cut two 10" pieces of ¼"-wide ribbon for straps. Place and pin gathered sleeve ruffles to underside of ribbon. Sew ribbon over gathered stitches.

10 Place and pin straps to outside of bib piece. Sew in place.

11 Center and pin bib to outside of waistband. Sew in place. Place and pin bottom end of straps to back of waistband. Sew in place.

12 Cut two 12" pieces of 1" ribbon. Sew ribbon ties to each end of waistband.

13 *Optional: Trim edges, with a ½" scalloped lace for a dressier look.*

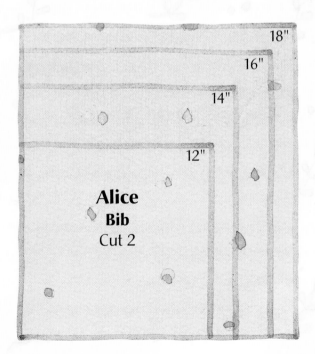

18"
16"
14"
12"

Alice
Bib
Cut 2

chapter 3

Winter Attire

Miss Rosie

Miss Rosie

Whether you are dressing a doll, teddy bear, or some other cuddly animal, a sweet dress adds so much to the character. This little bear loves her lavender and pink dress.

Fabric:

Fabric: cotton (¼ yd.)
        cotton (⅓ yd.)

Notions:

Buttons: ⅜" (3)
Fusible hem tape (optional)
Ribbon: ⅛"-wide (1 yd.)
Thread

Tools:

Fabric scissors
Iron and ironing board
Measuring tape
Sewing machine
Sewing needle
Straight pins
Tracing paper and pencil

Instructions for Dress

1 Refer to *Essential Basics* on pages 8–15. Using patterns on pages 98–99, trace patterns onto tracing paper. Place and pin dress pattern to ⅓ yd. cotton fabric. See Skirt Dimensions below. Cut or tear rectangle for skirt. See Bias Dimensions below. Using fabric scissors, cut bias strip. cut out pattern pieces. See Ruffle Dimensions on page 99. Cut two strips for ruffle from ¼ yd. cotton fabric.

2 Using sewing machine, sew shoulder seams, with right sides together. Using iron, press seams open.

3 Sew bias strip to neck edge, with right sides together. Fold bias strip in half to inside of neck edge. Refer to *Stitch Guide* on page 14. Using needle and thread, hand-stitch in place with overcast stitch.

4 Pin wrist end of sleeve in ½" and press. Machine-stitch, hand-stitch, or fuse (referring to *NoSew Instructions* on page 15) in place.

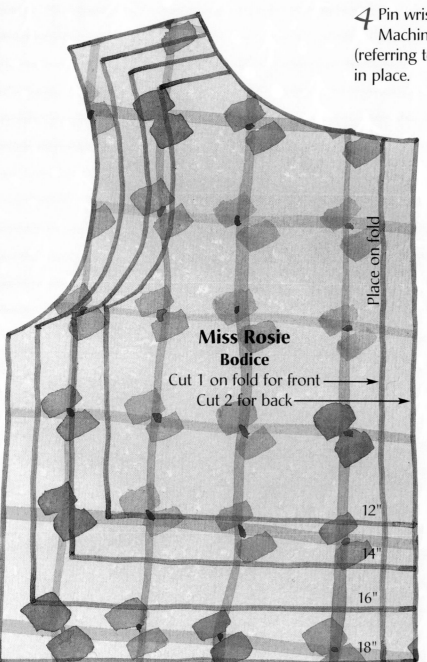

Place on fold

Miss Rosie
Bodice
Cut 1 on fold for front ⟶
Cut 2 for back ⟶

12"

14"

16"

18"

Bias Dimensions:

12"	5¼" x 1¼"
14"	6¼" x 1¼"
16"	8" x 1½"
18"	9½" x 1½"

Skirt Dimensions:

12"	24¼" x 5"
14"	28¼" x 5⅝"
16"	32" x 6⅜"
18"	36" x 7"

5 Sew running stitch across top of sleeve to help ease sleeve into armhole. Center and pin top of sleeve to shoulder seam, with right sides together. Sew from center out. Repeat for second sleeve.

6 Sew side seams of bodice and sleeves, with right sides together. Press seams open.

7 Sew two pieces of ruffle, with right sides together, forming one long ruffle. Fold one long edge of ruffle in ¼" and press. Sew or fuse in place.

8 Sew one long raw edge of ruffle with gathering stitch. Pull bobbin thread to gather.

9 Place and pin gathered ruffle to bottom of skirt, with right sides together. Sew in place.

10 Sew top of skirt with two rows of gathering stitches. Pull bobbin threads to gather. Center and pin skirt to bodice, with right sides together. Sew in place.

11 Sew center back edges of skirt, with right sides together, stopping 3" below bodice.

12 Fold center back opening in ⅜" and press to hold. Sew or fuse in place.

13 Using needle and thread, hand-stitch one button at back neck edge, midway back bodice, and waist. Cut six 6" ribbons. Machine-stitch or hand-stitch two ribbons opposite buttons on opposite side of bodice. Tie ribbons around buttons to secure dress.

Ruffle Dimensions:

12"	19" x 2¼"
14"	22" x 2¼"
16"	25¾" x 2½"
18"	28" x 2½"

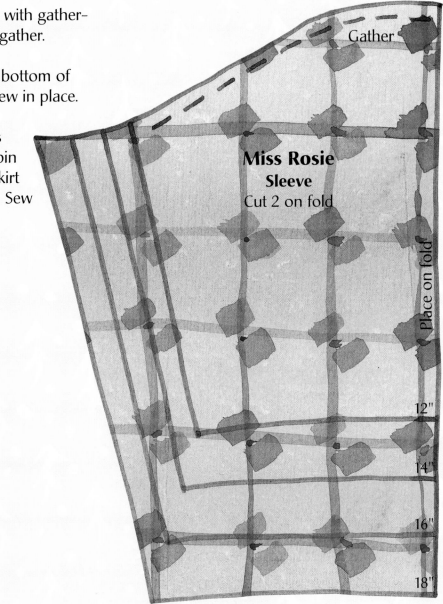

Gather

Miss Rosie
Sleeve
Cut 2 on fold

Place on fold

12"

14"

16"

18"

Audrey

Audrey

The jacket and skirt are sewn from a soft plaid wool, with sleeves and hem trimmed in old lace for a nostalgic charm.

Accessorize with lace about the neck and a tiny silk flower.

Fabric:

Fabric: lightweight wool (⅓ yd.)

Notions:

Buttons: ⅜" (5)
Fusible hem tape (optional)
Hooks and eyes (4)
Lace: 2"-wide (1¼ yd.)
Ribbon: ⅛"-wide satin (⅓ yd.)
Thread

Tools:

Fabric scissors
Iron and ironing board
Measuring tape
Sewing machine
Sewing needle
Straight pins
Tracing paper and pencil

Instructions for Jacket and Skirt

1 Refer to *Essential Basics* on pages 8–15. Using patterns on pages 102–105, trace patterns onto tracing paper. Place and pin patterns to wool fabric. Using fabric scissors, cut out pattern pieces. Using measuring tape, determine doll waist circumference, plus 1". Cut one 2"-wide strip to these dimensions for skirt waistband.

Jacket

1 Mark darts on all jacket fronts. Using sewing machine, sew in place.

2 Place and pin jacket fronts, with right sides together. Sew along neck edge, down front edge, and around bottom front. Turn right side out. Repeat for other side. Using iron, press jacket front. Press lapel back and set aside.

3 Place and pin jacket backs, with right sides together. Sew along neck edge. Sew bottom edge. Turn right side out and press.

4 Sew front and back shoulder seams, with right sides together. Press shoulder seams flat.

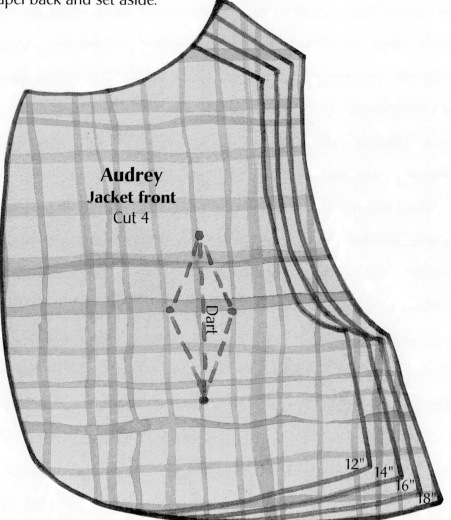

Audrey
Jacket front
Cut 4

Dart

12" 14" 16" 18"

5 Sew top of sleeve with gathering stitches. Pull bobbin thread to gather.

6 Turn wrist end of sleeve under ⅜" and machine-stitch or hand-stitch in place. *Optional: Refer to NoSew Instructions on page 15. Using iron, fuse cuff with fusible hem tape. Sew or fuse 2"-wide lace to inside edge of sleeve.*

7 Center and pin gathered sleeve to shoulder seam, with right sides together. Sew sleeve from center out. Repeat for second sleeve.

8 Sew side seams of jacket and sleeves, with right sides together.

9 Using needle and thread, hand-stitch hooks and eyes to front of jacket, allowing ⅜" overlap. Hand-stitch four buttons to front of jacket for decoration.

10 *Optional: Determine doll neck circumference, plus 2." Cut lace to these dimensions. Wrap around doll's neck and tuck into front of jacket.*

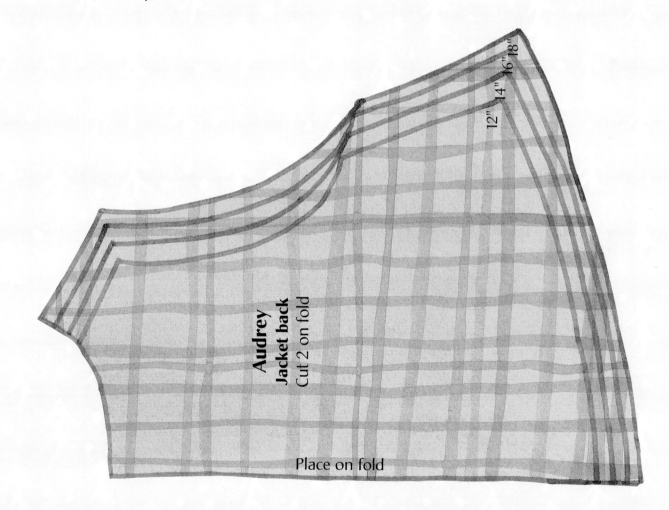

**Audrey
Jacket back
Cut 2 on fold**

12" 14" 16" 18"

Place on fold

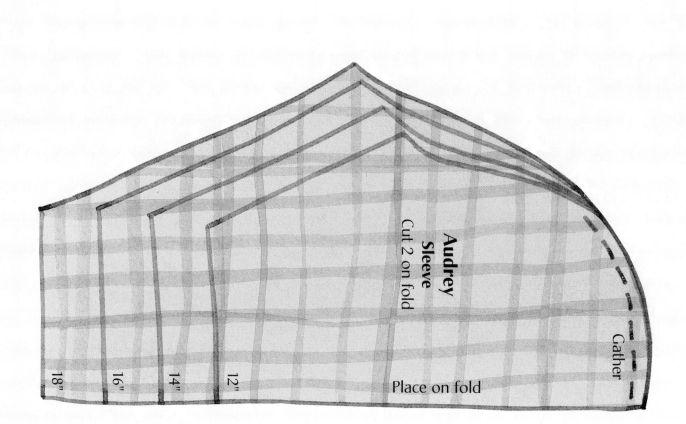

Audrey
Sleeve
Cut 2 on fold

Gather

Place on fold

18" 16" 14" 12"

Skirt

1 Using sewing machine, sew skirt pieces, with right sides together, leaving one seam open. See Illustration #1. Sew top of skirt with two rows of gathering stitches. Pull bobbin threads to gather.

2 Place and pin skirt to waistband, leaving ½" seam allowance at each end. Sew in place. Fold waistband in half to inside of skirt. Machine-stitch, hand-stitch, or fuse (referring to *NoSew Instructions* on page 15) in place.

3 Sew lace hem tape to bottom of skirt. Sew back seam of skirt, with right sides together, stopping 3" below waist. Fold seam of skirt and waistband in, and press. Machine-stitch, hand-stitch, or fuse in place.

Illustration #1

4 Place skirt on doll and mark hem at desired length. Remove skirt from doll and hem. Machine-stitch, hand-stitch, or bond lace to underside of hem, allowing lace to extend below hemline.

5 Using needle and thread, hand-stitch two buttons vertically to one end of waistband. Cut two 6" ribbons. Machine-stitch or hand-stitch ribbons to opposite end of waistband. Tie ribbons around buttons to secure waist.

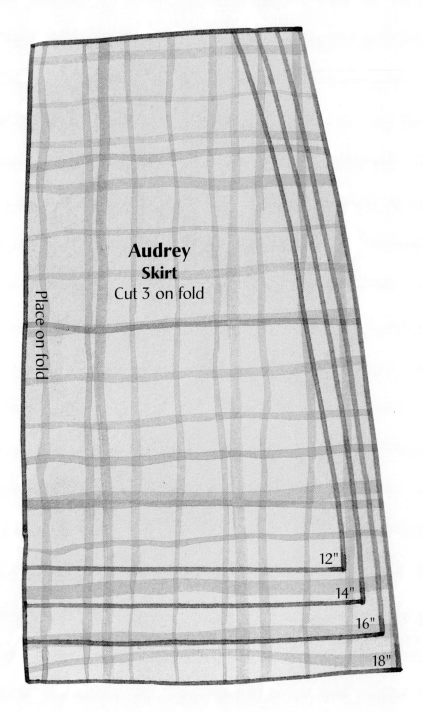

Place on fold

Audrey
Skirt
Cut 3 on fold

12"

14"

16"

18"

Joanie

Joanie

During the Victorian era, this dress would have been ideal for greeting visitors in the sitting room. Pretty details and body are added with pin tucks around the the skirt. A coordinating fabric adorns the neckline.

Fabric:

Fabric: cotton (½ yd.)
       cotton (scrap)

Notions:

Fusible hem tape (optional)
Thread
Velcro® tabs

Tools:

Fabric scissors
Iron and ironing board
Measuring tape
Sewing machine
Straight pins
Tracing paper and pencil

Instructions for Dress

1 Refer to *Essential Basics* on pages 8–15. Using patterns on pages 108–109, trace patterns onto tracing paper. Place and pin dress pattern to ½ yd. cotton fabric. See Skirt Dimensions on page 109. Cut or tear rectangle for skirt. Using fabric scissors, cut out pattern pieces. See Bias Dimensions on page 109. Cut bias strip from scrap cotton fabric for neck edge.

2 See Tuck Chart below. Using iron, press first tuck below top edge of skirt piece, following Tuck Chart. Using straight pins, pin and tuck ½" from fold and press. Using sewing machine, sew tuck in place. Press second tuck below first tuck and press. Pin and sew in place. Repeat for third and fourth tucks. Turn hem under, 1" below fourth tuck, and machine-stitch, hand-stitch, or fuse (referring to *NoSew Instructions* on page 15) with fusible hem tape.

3 Sew seam down front bodice pieces, with right sides together.

4 Sew shoulder seams, with right sides together. Using iron, press seams open.

5 Sew bias strip to neck edge, with right sides together. Fold bias strip in half to inside of neck edge and sew in place.

Tuck Chart

	12"	14"	16"	18"
1st tuck	2¼"	2¾"	3⅛"	3½"
2nd, 3rd & 4th tucks	1"	1¼"	1½"	2"
Hem	1¼"	1¼"	1½"	2"

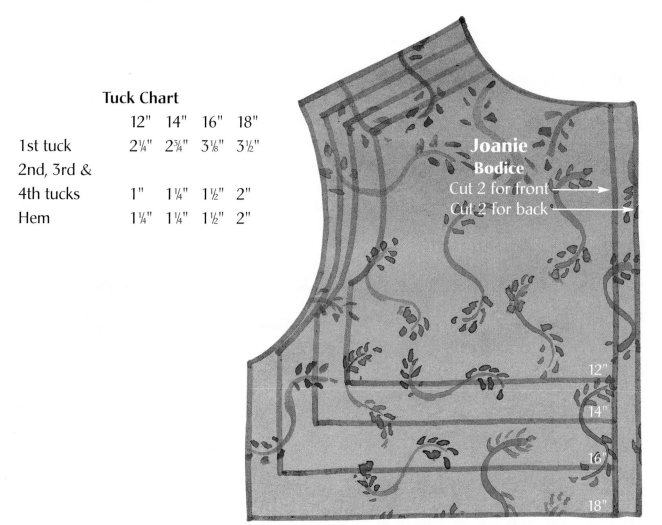

Joanie
Bodice
Cut 2 for front ⟶
Cut 2 for back ⟶

12"
14"
16"
18"

6 Fold wrist end of sleeve in ½" and press. Machine-stitch, hand-stitch, or fuse in place.

7 Sew running stitch across top of sleeve to help ease sleeve into armhole. Center and pin top of sleeve to shoulder seam with right sides together. Sew from center out. Repeat for second sleeve.

8 Sew bodice and sleeve seams, with right sides together. Press seams open.

9 Sew top of skirt with two rows of gathering stitch. Pull bobbin threads to gather. Center and pin skirt and bodice, with right sides together. Sew in place.

10 Sew center back edges of skirt, with right sides together, stopping 2" below bodice.

11 Fold center back opening in ⅜" and press. Sew or fuse in place. Attach Velcro tabs for closures.

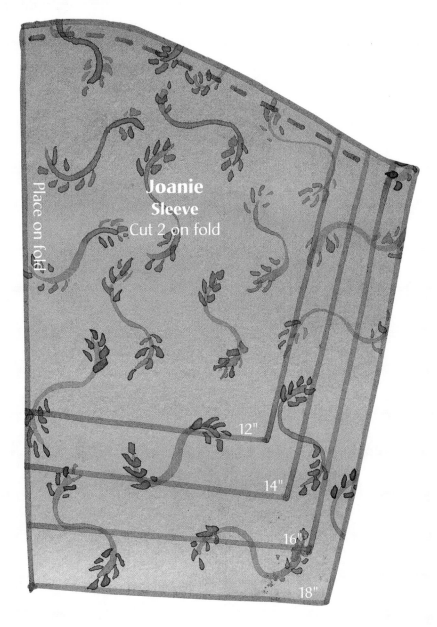

Place on fold

Joanie
Sleeve
Cut 2 on fold

12"
14"
16"
18"

Bias Dimensions:

12"	4¾" x 1½"
14"	5¼" x 1½"
16"	6¼" x 1½"
18"	7¼" x 1½"

Skirt Dimensions:

12"	16¼" x 11⅜"
14"	18⅞" x 12½"
16"	21½" x 13⅝"
18"	24" x 14⅝"

Jennifer

Jennifer

Mixing several patterned cotton and flannel fabrics results in an adorable dress and pantaloons with fresh-from-the-country charm.

Fabric:

Fabric: cotton, two contrasting patterns
        (¼ yd. each)
        cotton (½ yd.)
        embroidered eyelet (¼ yd.)
        flannel (¼ yd.)
        flannel (½ yd.)

Notions:

Drawstring (½ yd.)
Elastic: ¼"-wide (optional)
Fusible webbing
Fusible hem tape (optional)
Lace: 1"-wide scalloped edge (2½ yds.)
Low-loft quilt batting (scrap) (optional)
Ribbon: ¼"-wide embroidered (⅓ yd.)
Thread
Velcro® tabs

Tools:

Fabric scissors
Iron and ironing board
Measuring tape
Sewing machine
Small safety pin
Straight pins
Tracing paper and pencil

Instructions for Dress and Pantaloons

1 Refer to *Essential Basics* on pages 8–15. Using patterns on pages 113–116, trace patterns onto tracing paper. Place and pin bodice pattern to ½ yd. flannel fabric. See Skirt Dimensions on page 115. Cut or tear rectangle from ½ yd. flannel for skirt. Place and pin sleeve pattern to contrasting ¼ yd. flannel fabric. Place and pin pantaloons pattern to ½ yd. cotton fabric. Place and pin sleeve trim pattern to ¼ yd. contrasting cotton fabric. See Patchwork Square Dimensions on page 114. Using fabric scissors, cut fourteen squares for patchwork hem from the various contrasting fabrics as desired. See Apron Dimensions on page 115. Cut rectangle from embroidered eyelet fabric for apron. Cut out pattern pieces.

Dress

1 See Illustration #1. Using sewing machine, sew patchwork squares together, alternating patterns, to create one long strip. Using iron, press seams flat.

2 Fold one long side of patchwork strip in ½" and press. Machine-stitch, hand-stitch, or fuse (referring to *NoSew Instructions* on page 15) with fusible hem tape. Sew lace to inside of hem.

3 Trace Large and Small heart patterns on page 114 onto paper side of fusible webbing. Turn hearts over and trace other side, making complete heart. Cut square around hearts. Using iron, fuse Large heart to same fabric as sleeve trim, following manufacturer's instructions. Fuse Small heart to same fabric as pantaloons. Cut out Large and Small hearts and remove paper backing. Place hearts as desired on bodice front and fuse.

4 *Optional: Cut quilt batting ⅜" larger than appliqué. Place or pin batting to inside of bodice behind appliqué. Refer to Stitch Guide on page 14. Using needle and thread, hand-stitch a long running stitch around outside edge of*

Illustration #1

batting. Quilt around outside of appliqué for added dimension and accent. Remove long running stitch.

5 Sew shoulder seams, with right sides together. Using iron, press seams open.

6 Fold neck edge in ⅜" and press. Machine-stitch, hand-stitch, or fuse with fusible hem

tape. Machine-stitch or hand-stitch lace to inside of neck edge.

7 Note: *Added trim may make sleeve too long for some dolls. Refer to Measuring Your Doll and Adjusting Patterns on page 9.* Place and pin sleeve trim piece to wrist end of sleeve, with right sides together. Sew in place. Fold sleeve trim in ½" and press. Machine-stitch or hand-stitch in place.

Gather

Place on fold

Jennifer
Sleeve
Cut 2 on fold

12"

14"

16"

18"

8 Place and pin lace to underside of sleeve trim. Sew in place. Place and pin ribbon to outside edge of sleeve. Sew in place. Repeat for second sleeve.

9 Sew top of sleeve pieces with gathering stitch. Pull bobbin thread to gather. Center and pin top of sleeve to shoulder seam, with right sides together. Machine-stitch or hand-stitch from center out. Repeat for second sleeve.

10 Sew bodice and sleeve seams, with right sides together.

11 Fold three sides of apron in ¼" and press. Sew in place. *Note: If a scalloped hem is used, only two sides will need to be sewn.*

12 Place and pin patchwork strip to one long side of skirt piece, with right sides together. Sew in place.

13 Sew top of skirt and raw edge of apron with two rows of gathering stitch. Pull bobbin threads to gather.

14 Center and pin apron on skirt. Center and pin skirt and apron to bodice, with right sides together. Sew in place.

15 Sew center back edges of skirt, with right sides together, stopping 3" below bodice.

16 Fold center back opening in ½" and press. Sew or fuse in place. Attach Velcro tabs for closures.

✔ *Two-hour assembly is based on sewing time of finished dress and not on quilting time. This dress may require extra time for quilting.*

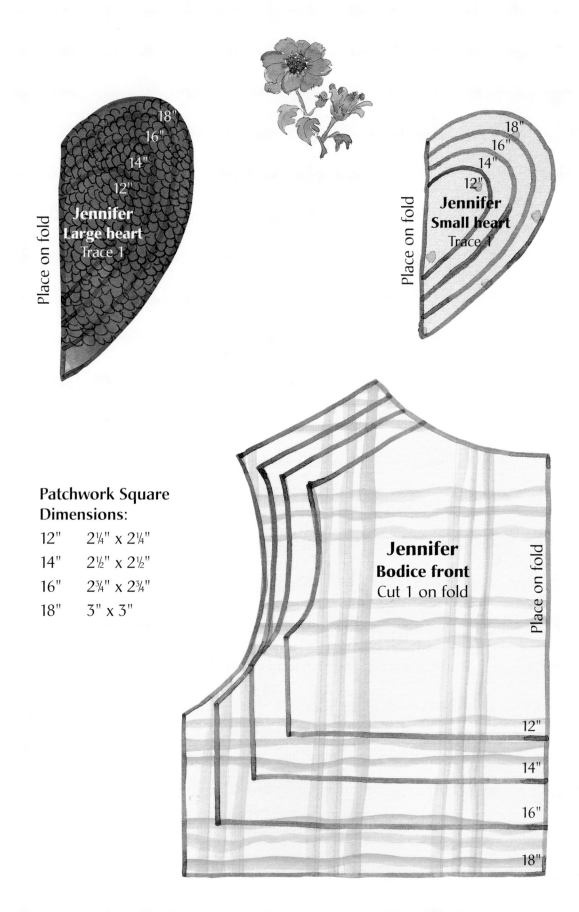

Jennifer
Large heart
Trace 1

Place on fold

18"
16"
14"
12"

Jennifer
Small heart
Trace 1

Place on fold

18"
16"
14"
12"

Patchwork Square
Dimensions:

12"	2¼" x 2¼"
14"	2½" x 2½"
16"	2¾" x 2¾"
18"	3" x 3"

Jennifer
Bodice front
Cut 1 on fold

Place on fold

12"
14"
16"
18"

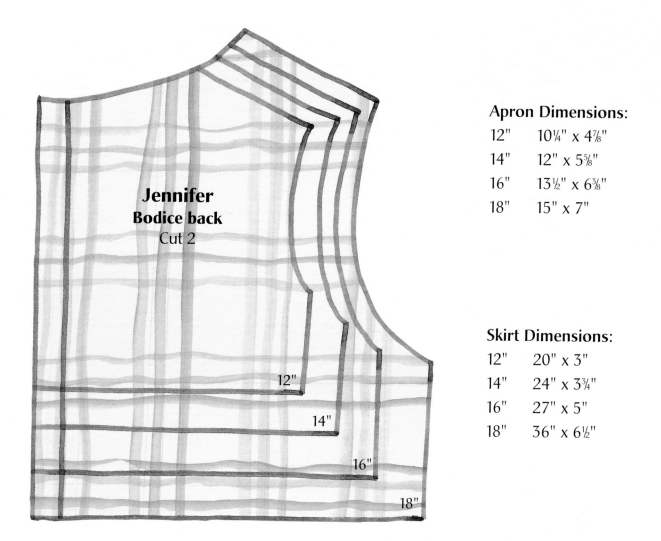

Jennifer
Bodice back
Cut 2

12"

14"

16"

18"

Apron Dimensions:

12"	10¼" x 4⅞"
14"	12" x 5⅝"
16"	13½" x 6⅜"
18"	15" x 7"

Skirt Dimensions:

12"	20" x 3"
14"	24" x 3¾"
16"	27" x 5"
18"	36" x 6½"

Pantaloons

1 Using sewing machine, sew front seam from "A" to "B" with right sides together. Repeat with back seam.

2 Fold bottom of pants in ½" and press. Sew lace to underside edge of hem. Sew second row of lace ½" from hemline to outside of hem.

3 Sew inside leg seam, with right sides together.

4 Fold top of pants in ½" and press. Sew casing ¼" from raw edge around top of pants, leaving 1" opening at back seam for drawstring. Attach safety pin to drawstring and push through casing. Place pants on doll and pull drawstring to fit waist. Tie in bow. *Optional: Elastic may be inserted into casing in place of drawstring.*

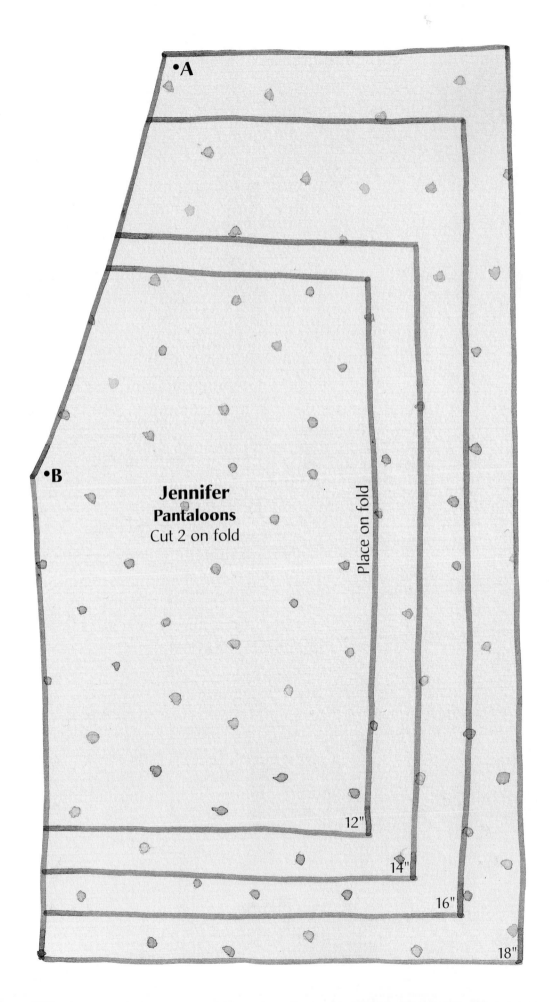

•A

•B

Jennifer
Pantaloons
Cut 2 on fold

Place on fold

12"

14"

16"

18"

Helen

Helen

A piece of soft wool and lovely braid trim set off this pretty jacket. Combine the jacket with a checked-cotton skirt trimmed with velvet, and you have the perfect traveling ensemble. The skirt could be made from wool for a business look.

Gathered skirts may also be made from pretty laces, cottons, velvets, and silks.

Fabric:

Fabric: cotton (⅛ yd.)
       wool (⅛ yd.)

Notions:

Braid ½"-wide (1¾ yd.)
Button: ⅜" (1)
Fabric glue (optional)
Fusible hem tape (optional)
Hem lace (optional)
Ribbon: 1"-wide grosgrain (⅖ yd.)
       ⅛"-wide velvet (1⅓ yds.)
       ¾"-wide velvet (½ yd.)
Thread

Tools:

Fabric glue (optional)
Fabric scissors
Iron and ironing board
Measuring tape
Sewing machine
Sewing needle
Straight pins
Tracing paper and pencil

Instructions for Jacket and Skirt

1 Refer to *Essential Basics* on pages 8–15. Using patterns on pages 119–121, trace patterns onto tracing paper. Place and pin jacket patterns to wool fabric. Using fabric scissors, cut out pattern pieces. See Skirt Dimensions on page 121. Cut rectangle from cotton fabric for skirt. Using measuring tape, determine doll waist circumference, plus 1". Cut 2"-wide strip to these dimensions for waistband.

Jacket

1 Using sewing machine, sew shoulder seams, with right sides together. Using iron, press seams open.

2 Mark back dart and sew in place. Fold neck edge in ⅜" and pin. Sew or fuse (referring to *NoSew Instructions* on page 15) in place.

3 Sew outside edges of collar, with right sides together. Turn right side out and, using iron, press flat.

4 Fold raw edge of collar in ⅜" and press. Center and pin collar to neck edge. Topstitch in place. Using needle and thread, hand-stitch or bond braid around outside edge of collar.

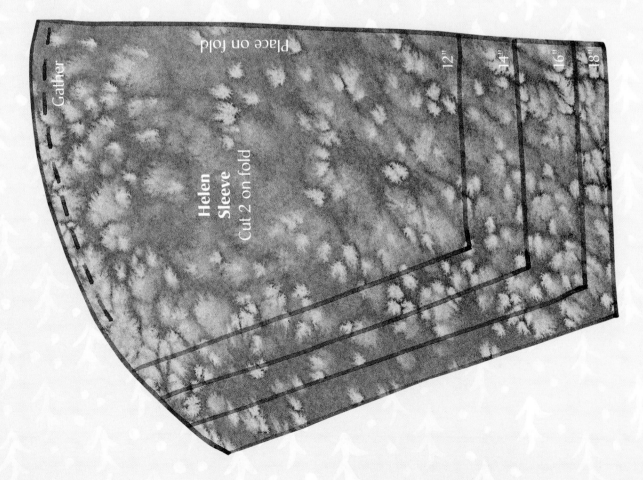

Gather

Place on fold

Helen
Sleeve
Cut 2 on fold

12" 14" 16" 18"

5 Place and pin ¾"-wide velvet ribbon to jacket front opening, with wrong sides together. Sew in place. Turn ribbon to outside of jacket and sew in place.

6 Fold and pin wrist end of sleeve in ½" and press. Sew in place. Hand-stitch or bond braid to wrist edge. Repeat for second sleeve.

7 Sew gathering stitch across top of sleeve to help ease sleeve into armhole. Center and pin sleeve to shoulder, with right sides together. Sew in place. Repeat for second sleeve.

8 Sew side seams of jacket and sleeves, with right sides together. Fold bottom edge of jacket in and sew or fuse in place. *Optional: Hem bottom edge of jacket with hem lace.* Hand-stitch or bond braid to hem of jacket.

9 Cut two 12" pieces of grosgrain ribbon for ties. Hand-stitch one ribbon to each side of front opening for closure.

Back dart for 12" & 14"

Back dart for 16" & 18"

Helen
Jacket
Cut 1 on fold for back
Cut 2 for front

Place on fold

12"

14"

16"

18"

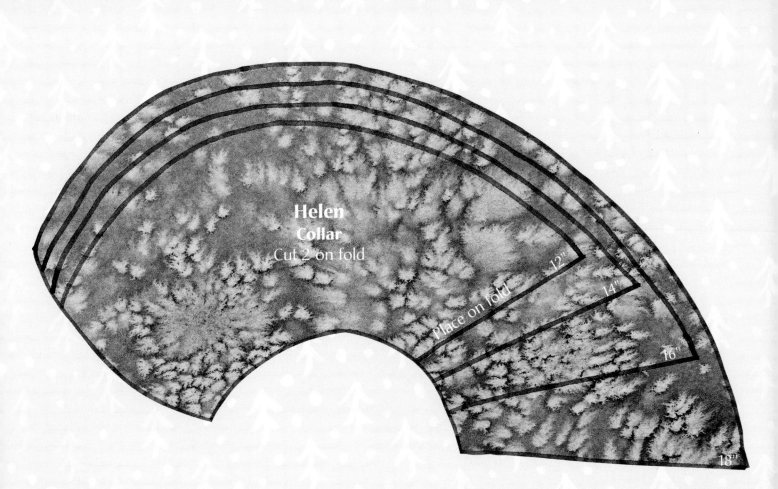

Helen
Collar
Cut 2 on fold

Place on fold

12"

14"

16"

18"

Skirt

1 Using sewing machine, sew ⅛"-wide ribbon onto skirt 6" from bottom edge of skirt. *Optional: Refer to NoSew Instructions on page 15. Ribbon may be fused to skirt with fusible web tape.*

2 Sew top of skirt with two rows of gathering stitch. Pull bobbin threads to gather. Place and pin skirt to waistband. Sew in place. Fold waistband edge ⅛" to inside, then fold ½" and press. Machine-stitch, hand-stitch, or fuse in place.

3 Sew back seam of skirt, with right sides together, stopping 2" below waist. Fold opening of skirt and waistband in ⅜" and press. Machine-stitch, hand-stitch, or fuse in place.

4 Turn bottom edge of skirt under to desired length and press. Machine-stitch, hand-stitch, or fuse hem in place.

5 Using needle and thread, hand-stitch button to one end of waistband. Cut two 6" pieces of ⅛"-wide ribbon. Machine-stitch or hand-stitch ribbons to opposite end of waistband. Tie ribbons around button to secure waist.

Skirt Dimensions:

12"	22¼" x 8⅛"
14"	25¾" x 9⅜"
16"	29½" x 10⅝"
18"	33" x 11⅞"

Gabriella

Gabriella

The idea for this cozy robe came about while buying one for myself. It looks very sweet on my teddy bear, and will look just as adorable and cuddly on any doll. The time necessary to construct this robe was under two hours.

Sew a coat with wool, fake fur, or leather, using this pattern. Shorten the pattern for a jacket.

Fabric:

Fabric: fleece (⅓ yd.)

Notions:

Ribbon: 1"-wide grosgrain (2 yds.)
        2"-wide (2 yds.)
Thread

Tools:

Fabric scissors
Measuring tape
Sewing machine
Straight pins
Tracing paper and pencil

Instructions for Robe

1 Refer to *Essential Basics* on pages 8–15. Using patterns on pages 124–125, trace patterns onto tracing paper. Tape robe pattern extension to robe pattern top. Place and pin robe pattern to fleece fabric. Using fabric scissors, cut out pattern pieces.

2 Using sewing machine, sew shoulder and top sleeve seams, with right sides together. Using hands, press seams open.

3 Sew 2"-wide ribbon, to neck and front opening, with right sides

together. Fold ribbon in half to inside of robe. Sew in place.

Note: Tape upper robe pattern to lower robe pattern before cutting fabric.

18"
16"
14"
12"

Gabriella
Upper robe
Cut 2 for front
Cut 1 on fold for back

Cut here for 12" & 14"
Cut here for 16"
Cut here for 18"

Place on fold

4 Sew 2"-wide ribbon to hem of robe, with right sides together. Fold ribbon in half to inside of hem. Sew in place.

5 See Illustration #1. Sew grosgrain ribbon, right side up, along seam edge of 2"-wide ribbon, leaving side away from opening unstitched.

6 Sew 2"-wide ribbon to wrist end of sleeve, with right sides together. Fold ribbon over to inside of sleeve. Sew in place. Repeat for second sleeve.

7 Sew side and sleeve seams, with right sides together. Press seams open.

Illustration #1

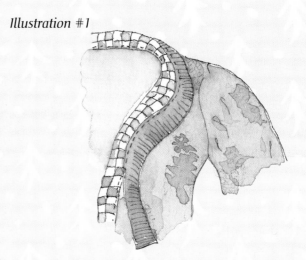

8 Use remaining grosgrain ribbon as belt for robe.

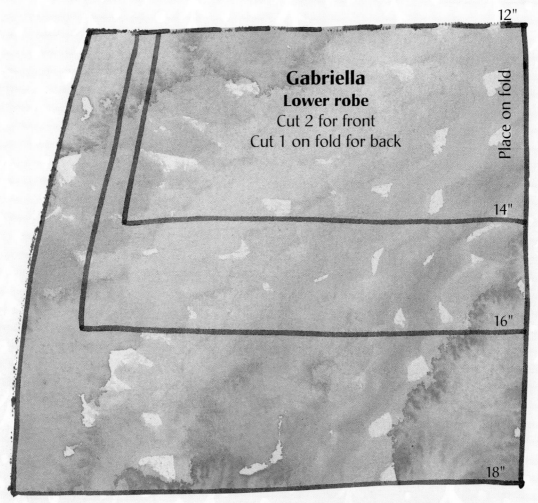

12"

Gabriella
Lower robe
Cut 2 for front
Cut 1 on fold for back

Place on fold

14"

16"

18"

Note: Tape lower robe pattern to upper robe pattern before cutting fabric.

Metric Equivalency Chart

mm–millimetres   cm–centimetres
inches to millimetres and centimetres

inches	mm	cm	inches	cm	inches	cm
1/8	3	0.3	9	22.9	30	76.2
1/4	6	0.6	10	25.4	31	78.7
3/8	10	1.0	11	27.9	32	81.3
1/2	13	1.3	12	30.5	33	83.8
5/8	16	1.6	13	33.0	34	86.4
3/4	19	1.9	14	35.6	35	88.9
7/8	22	2.2	15	38.1	36	91.4
1	25	2.5	16	40.6	37	94.0
1 1/4	32	3.2	17	43.2	38	96.5
1 1/2	38	3.8	18	45.7	39	99.1
1 3/4	44	4.4	19	48.3	40	101.6
2	51	5.1	20	50.8	41	104.1
2 1/2	64	6.4	21	53.3	42	106.7
3	76	7.6	22	55.9	43	109.2
3 1/2	89	8.9	23	58.4	44	111.8
4	102	10.2	24	61.0	45	114.3
4 1/2	114	11.4	25	63.5	46	116.8
5	127	12.7	26	66.0	47	119.4
6	152	15.2	27	68.6	48	121.9
7	178	17.8	28	71.1	49	124.5
8	203	20.3	29	73.7	50	127.0

yards to metres

yards	metres	yards	metres	yards	metres	yards	metres	yards	metres
1/8	0.11	2 1/8	1.94	4 1/8	3.77	6 1/8	5.60	8 1/8	7.43
1/4	0.23	2 1/4	2.06	4 1/4	3.89	6 1/4	5.72	8 1/4	7.54
3/8	0.34	2 3/8	2.17	4 3/8	4.00	6 3/8	5.83	8 3/8	7.66
1/2	0.46	2 1/2	2.29	4 1/2	4.11	6 1/2	5.94	8 1/2	7.77
5/8	0.57	2 5/8	2.40	4 5/8	4.23	6 5/8	6.06	8 5/8	7.89
3/4	0.69	2 3/4	2.51	4 3/4	4.34	6 3/4	6.17	8 3/4	8.00
7/8	0.80	2 7/8	2.63	4 7/8	4.46	6 7/8	6.29	8 7/8	8.12
1	0.91	3	2.74	5	4.57	7	6.40	9	8.23
1 1/8	1.03	3 1/8	2.86	5 1/8	4.69	7 1/8	6.52	9 1/8	8.34
1 1/4	1.14	3 1/4	2.97	5 1/4	4.80	7 1/4	6.63	9 1/4	8.46
1 3/8	1.26	3 3/8	3.09	5 3/8	4.91	7 3/8	6.74	9 3/8	8.57
1 1/2	1.37	3 1/2	3.20	5 1/2	5.03	7 1/2	6.86	9 1/2	8.69
1 5/8	1.49	3 5/8	3.31	5 5/8	5.14	7 5/8	6.97	9 5/8	8.80
1 3/4	1.60	3 3/4	3.43	5 3/4	5.26	7 3/4	7.09	9 3/4	8.92
1 7/8	1.71	3 7/8	3.54	5 7/8	5.37	7 7/8	7.20	9 7/8	9.03
2	1.83	4	3.66	6	5.49	8	7.32	10	9.14

Index